Apple 2020 Ma User Guide

The Complete Beginner to Expert Guide to Maximizing your 2020 MacBook Air

Andrew O. Murphy

Copyright © 2020 by Andrew O. Murphy - All rights reserved.

No part of this publication may be reproduced, stored in a retrieval system or transmitted in any form or by any means, electronic, mechanical, photocopying, recording, and scanning without permission in writing by the author.

CONTENTS

INTRODUCTION 1

CHAPTER 1 4

TAKE A TOUR OF YOUR NEW MACBOOK AIR: 4

What's included 5

MacBook Air Magic Keyboard with Touch ID 6

MacBook Air trackpad 9

Charge the MacBook Air battery 11

MacBook Air accessories 12

Work with wireless accessories 13

Use an external display with your MacBook Air 14

CHAPTER 2 16

HOW TO GET STARTED: 16

Set up your Mac 16

Apple Account on Mac 20

The desktop, menu bar, and Help on your Mac 23

The Finder on your Mac 24

The Dock on your Mac 27

Notification Center on your Mac 27

System Preferences on your Mac 28

Spotlight on your Mac 29

Siri on your Mac 32

Quickly open apps on your Mac 35

Display settings for your Mac 36

Transfer your data to your new MacBook Air 38

Back up and restore your Mac 40

CHAPTER 3 43

USE MACBOOK AIR WITH OTHER DEVICES: 43

Access your iCloud content on your Mac 43

Use Handoff on your Mac 46

Use Universal Clipboard on your Mac 47

Continuity Camera on your Mac 48

Continuity Sketch and Continuity Markup on your Mac 51

AirDrop on your Mac 52

Phone calls and text messages on your Mac 54

Instant Hotspot on your Mac 55

Unlock your Mac and approve tasks with Apple Watch 56

Use Apple Pay on your Mac 59

Use AirPlay on your Mac... 60

Use AirPrint on your Mac 62

CHAPTER 4 62

APPS INCLUDED WITH YOUR MAC: 63

App Store 64

Books 65

Calendar 67

FaceTime.. 69

Find My 71

GarageBand 73

Home 75

iMovie 76

Keynote 78

Mail 80

Maps 83

Maps 84

Messages 86

Music 88

News 90

Notes 91

Numbers 93

Pages 95

Photos 97

Podcasts 99

Reminders 100

Safari 103

Stocks 107

TV 109

Voice Memos 110

Keyboard shortcuts on your Mac 111

Save space on your MacBook Air 113

Take a screenshot on your Mac 116

CHAPTER 5 118

MAXIMIZING THE APPS: 118

Apps included on your Mac 118

Use Launchpad to view and open apps on Mac 118

Removeoapps from Launchpad 120

Manage windows on Mac 120

Use apps in full screen on Mac 123

Use apps in Split View on Mac 125

Find, buy, and download apps in the App Store on Mac 127

Install and reinstall apps purchased from the App Store on Mac 129

Reinstall apps that came with your mac 131

Install and uninstall apps from the internet or disc on Mac 132

CHAPTER 6 .... **134**

CUSTOMIZE YOUR MAC: **134**

Customize your Mac with System Preferences 134

Customize the desktop picture on your Mac 137

Use your internet accounts on Mac 140

Set up Screen Time for yourself on Mac 144

Change the appearance of the desktop 146

Use accessibility features on Mac 151

Control the pointer and mouse actions using alternate methods ... 153

Change how your keyboard, mouse, and trackpad work 154

Control your Mac with assistive devices 154

Change people's pictures in apps on Mac 155

Your user picture 156

Your picture in Messages 156

Your picture in Mail 156

Picturesoin Contacts 156

Set up users, guests, and groups on Mac 157

Add a user 157

Create a group 159

Convert a standard user to an administrator 160

Let occasional users log in as guests 161

Customize the login experience 162

Run Windows on your Mac 163

CHAPTER 7 165

WORK WITH FILES AND FOLDERS: 165

Create and work with documents on Mac 165

Create documents 166

Format documents 166

Save documents 167

Find documents 168

Dictate your messages and documents on Mac 169

Turn on keyboard dictation 170

Dictate text 170

Set a different keyboard dictation shortcut 171

Change the microphone used for keyboard dictation 172

Turn off keyboard dictation 172

Take screenshots or screen recordings on mac **172**

Take pictures or screen recordings using Screenshot 173

Take pictures using keyboard shortcuts 175

View and edit files with Quick Look on Mac 177

Mark up files on Mac 179

Combine files into a PDF on Mac 186

Print documents from your Mac 187

Organize files in stacks on Mac 189

Use stacks on the desktop 189

Use stacks in the Dock 191

Organize files in folders on Mac 193

Create a folder 193

Move items into folders 193

Quickly group multiple items into a new folder 194

Merge two folders with the same name 195

Use tags to organize files on Mac 195

Tag files and folders 195

Find items you tagged 196

Remove tags 197

Edit tags 198

Back up your files with Time Machine on Mac 199

Restore items backed up with Time Machine on Mac 201

CHAPTER 8 .... **204**

APPLE ID AND ICLOUD **204**

Create an Apple ID on Mac 204

Use two-factor authentication for security on your Mac, iOS devices, and iPadOS devices 205

Turn on two-factor authentication for your Apple ID 206

Sign in to a new device or browser with two-factor authentication 206

Get a verification code on a Mac, even when it's offline 207

Add a trusted device 208

Add or remove a trusted phone number 209

View or remove trusted devices 209

Set up your Apple ID preferences 210

Set up iCloud features on Mac 212

Turn iCloud features on or off 213

Turn on iCloud Photos 214

Change iCloud Keychain options 214

Change Find My Mac details 215

Use iCloud Drive to store documents on your Mac, iPhone, and iPad 216

Set up iCloud Drive 216

Store your Desktop and Documents folders in iCloud Drive 217

If you can't move or save a document to iCloud Drive 218

Use iCloud File Sharing to share documents with other iCloud users 219

Share documents 219

Accept an invitation and revise a document 221

Change the sharing options of a document 222

Stop sharing a document 223

Use iCloud File Sharing to share documents with other iCloud users 224

Share documents 224

Accept an invitation and revise a document..................................... 226

Change the sharing options of a document 227

Stop sharing a document 228

Manage iCloud storage on Mac 229

View and manage iCloud storage 229

Delete items from iCloud storage 231

Use iCloud Photos to store photos in iCloud 231

Turn on iCloud Photos 232

Stop using iCloud Photos 234

CHAPTER 9 236

FAMILY AND FRIENDS: 236

Set up Family Sharing on Mac 236

Set up Screen Time for a child on Mac... 240

Share purchases with others in your Family Sharing group 242

View and download purchases made by other family members 243

Hide a purchase from other family members 244

Stop hiding a purchase 245

Stop sharing your purchases 246

Ways to share calendars on Mac 246

Share your calendar with friends and family 246

ix

Share your calendar with coworkers 246

Share a read-only version of your calendar with anyone 247

Stop sharing a calendar 247

Share a reminder list on Mac 247

Share a list 248

Add people to a shared list.. 248

Remove people from a shared list 249

Stop sharing a list 250

Create a shared album in Photos on Mac 250

Create a shared album.. 251

View a shared album 251

Stop sharing an album 251

View activity in your shared albums 252

LOCATE A FRIEND IN FIND MY ON MAC 253

CHAPTER 10.. 255

PRIVACY AND SECURITY 255

Learn how passwords are used on 255

Login password 255

Apple ID 255

Passwords in iCloud Keychain 256

Passwords in Keychain Access 256

Recovery key 257

Manage passwords using keychains on Mac....................................257

What is a keychain? 257

x

Keychain Access..258

ICloud Keychain 259

Reset your Mac login password 260

Reset your login password using your Apple ID 260

Reset your login password using a recovery key............................ 260

Reset the password of another user... 261

Set up your Mac to be secure 261

Use secure passwords.. 261

Require users to log in... 262

Secure your Mac when it's idle 262

Limit the number of administrative users 262

Encrypt the data on your Mac with File Vault 263

Guard your privacy on Mac...263

Use Screen Time 263

Use the privacy features in Safari 263

Control the personal information you share with apps 264

Choose whether to share analytics information 264

Set up a firewall 265

Protect your Mac from malware 265

Use Sign in with Apple on Mac.. 267

Create an account for an app or website.. 267

Sign in to your account for an app or website 268

Change the address used to forward email from apps and websites
.... 268

xi

Change Sign in with Apple settings for an app or website............... 269
Clear your browsing history in Safari on Mac................................... 269
Manage cookies and website data in Safari on Mac 271
Locate a device in Find My on Mac 272
See the location of a device 272
Play a sound on a device 272
Get directions to a device...273

Introduction

The MacBook Air (2020) addresses a number of complaints we've had about previous releases of Apple's affordable thin and light laptop. Our biggest issue with previous models was how the hardware powering them was beginning to feel rather outdated and under powered, especially compared to many Windows-based laptops of around the same price tag.

While Apple was understandably trying to make the MacBook Air as affordable as possible, we felt there were a few too many compromises, especially when it came to processing power and storage space. Plus, each yearly update felt like a small step up, rather than a revolutionary jump.

The good news is that the MacBook Air 2020 feels like a much bigger step up from the MacBook Air 2019, with Apple finally adding new components that gives it a decent uptick in performance. It's also upped the minimum storage capacity of the device (it now starts at 256GB, rather than the paltry 128GB of previous models), and for the first time offers configurations with quad-core processors and up to 16GB of RAM.

It does all of this without neglecting that all-important thin and light design which the MacBook Air is famous for. While it's not the thinnest laptop around (the LG Gram, for instance, is one of several Windows 10 laptops that weighs less than the MacBook Air these days), it's still an impressively compact laptop with

Apple's famous design and build quality, and while the new components add a little extra size and weight to the overall dimensions of the new MacBook Air, it's remains a laptop you can easily and comfortably carry around with you.

When it comes to price, Apple has pleasantly surprised us by releasing the MacBook Air 2020 at a starting price that's lower than what the 2019 model launched at: $999 / £999 / AU$1,599. Not only is this cheaper, but the specs are better than last year's model, with the entry-level model featuring a dual-core 10th-generation 1.1GHz Intel Core i3 processor with a boost of 3.2GHz, 256GB storage and 8GB of LPDDR4X RAM.

Design-wise, things are pretty much the same, but with one major (and welcome) difference: the MacBook Air 2020 comes with a new keyboard. Gone is the old butterfly switches, which were too shallow for many people, and prone to failing if debris, such as dust and crumbs, fell between the keys, and in its place is the new Magic keyboard, which first appeared with the MacBook Pro 16-inch. This offers a deeper travel when typing, so it feels more responsive, and – crucially – it appears to have fixed the reliability issues of the older keyboard.

Elsewhere, it's pretty much business as usual, which is good news if you love Apple's devices and have been hankering after a MacBook Air that performs as well as it looks. However, if

Apple's laptops have previously left you cold, then there's not much here that will make you change your mind.

Chapter 1
Take a tour of your new MacBook Air

Note: This guide is for the 13-inch MacBook Air with Retina display. The MacBook Air has the following features built in:

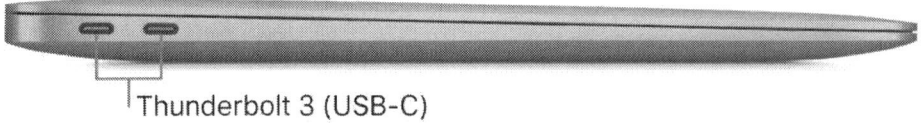
Thunderbolt 3 (USB-C)

- *Thunderbolt 3 (USB-C) ports:* Charge your computer, transfer data at Thunderbolt speeds (up to 40 Gbps), connect to a display or projector, and more.

3.5 mm headphone jack

- *3.5 mm headphone jack:* Plug in stereo headphones or external speakers to listen to your favorite music or movies.

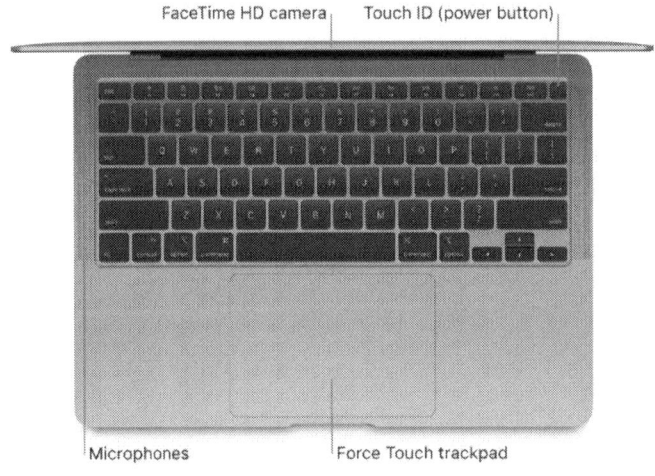

- *FaceTime HD camera:* Make FaceTime video calls or take pictures and video. If the light is glowing, the camera is on.

- *Touc ID (the power button):* Press to turn on your MacBook Air (or just lift the lid). When you first start up or restart, you need to log in by typing your password. After you set up Touch ID, you can authenticate with a touch instead of typing your password (after your first login), and use Touch ID for Apple Pay purchases. *Microphones:* Talk with friends or record audio with multiple built-in microphones.

- *Force Touch trackpad:* Control your MacBook Air with gestures. The entire trackpad surface acts as a button so you can easily click anywhere.

What's included

- To use your MacBook Air, you need these two accessories, included in the box:

Accessory	Description
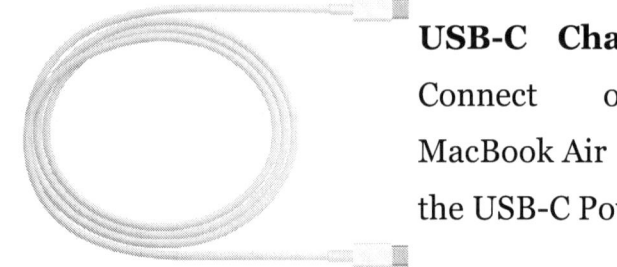	**USB-C Charge Cable (2 m):** Connect one end to your MacBook Air and the other end to the USB-C Power Adapter.

Accessory	Description
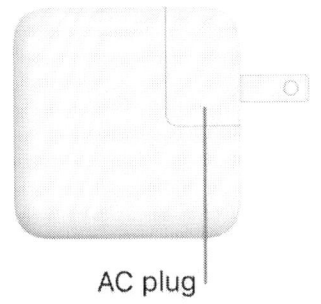 AC plug	**30W USB-C Power Adapter:** To charge your MacBook Air, fully extend the electrical prongs on the AC plug, and plug the adapter into an AC power outlet.

- Other adapters and accessories are sold separately. Visit apple.com, your local Apple Store, or other resellers for more information and availability. Review the documentation or check with the manufacturer to make sure you choose the right product.

MacBook Air Magic Keyboard with Touch ID

The function keys along the upper edge of the Magic Keyboard keyboard provide shortcuts for common functions, such as increasing the volume or screen brightness. Touch ID (the power button) is located on the right side of the function keys. After you set up Touch ID, you can use your fingerprint to unlock MacBook Air and make purchases from the App Store, Apple TV app, and Book Store, and on websites using Apple Pay.

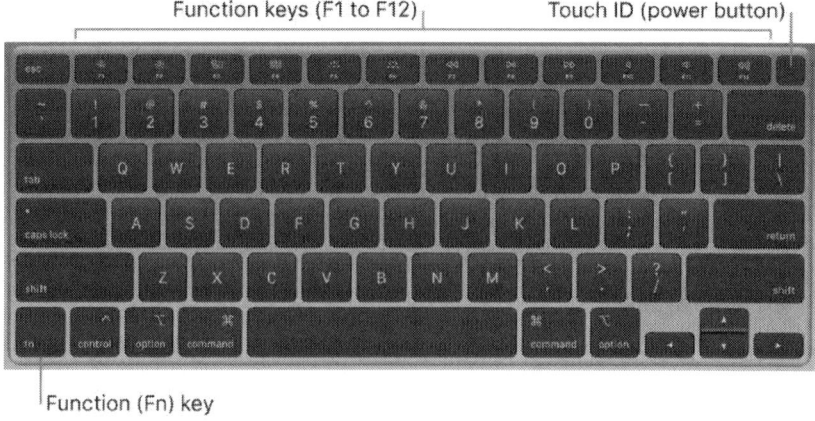

Function (Fn) key

Touch ID (power button): Press to turn on your MacBook Air (or just lift the lid or press any key). When you first start up or restart the computer, you need to log in by typing your password. You can set up Touch ID during setup, or later in the Touch ID pane of System Preferences. After setup and initial login, whenever you're asked for your password, you can just place your finger lightly on the Touch ID sensor to authenticate. You can also use Touch ID to make online purchases securely with Apple Pay. *Note:* To turn off your MacBook Air, choose Apple menu > Shut Down. To put your MacBook Air to sleep, choose Apple menu > Sleep. Many system functions can be accessed through the function keys.

- *Brightness keys (F1, F2):* Press or to decrease or increase the brightness of the screen.

- *Mission Control key (F3):* Press ⌘ to view what's running on your MacBook Air, including all your spaces and open windows.

- *Launchpad key (F4):* Press ▦ to instantly see all the apps on your MacBook Air. Click an app to open it.

- *Keyboard illumination keys (F5, F6):* Press ☼ or ☼ to decrease or increase the brightness of the keyboard.

- *Media keys (F7, F8, F9):* Press ◁◁ to rewind, ▷‖ to play or pause, or ▷▷ to fast-forward a song, movie, or slideshow.

- *Mute key (F10):* Press 🔇 to mute the sound from the built-in speakers or 3.5 mm headphone jack.

- *Volume keys (F11, F12):* Press 🔉 or 🔊 to decrease or increase the volume of sound from the built-in speakers or 3.5 mm headphone jack.

- *Function (Fn) key:* Each function key (on the top row) can also perform other functions—for example, the F11 key can hide all open windows and show the desktop. Hold down the Fn key while you press a function key to trigger the action associated with the key.

Tip: Press the Fn key twice to turn on dictation, which lets you dictate text wherever you can type (for example, in Messages, Mail, Pages, and many other apps).

Set keyboard preferences. In System Preferences, click Keyboard, then click the buttons at the top to see the available options.

MacBook Air trackpad

You can do a lot on your MacBook Air using simple trackpad gestures—scroll through webpages, zoom in on documents, rotate photos, and more. With the Force Touch trackpad, pressure-sensing capabilities add another level of interactivity. The trackpad provides feedback—when you drag or rotate objects, you feel a subtle vibration when they're aligned, allowing you to work with greater precision.

Here are some common gestures:

Gesture Action

Click: Press anywhere on the trackpad. Or enable "Tap to click" in Trackpad preferences, and simply tap.

Force click: Click and then press deeper. You can use force click to look up more information—click a word to see its definition, or an address to see a preview that you can open in Maps.

Gesture Action

Secondary click (that is, right-click): Click with two fingers to open shortcut menus. If "Tap to click" is enabled, tap with two fingers.

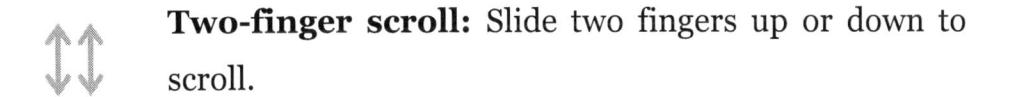

Two-finger scroll: Slide two fingers up or down to scroll.

Pinch to zoom: Pinch your thumb and finger open or closed to zoom in or out of photos and webpages.

Swipe to navigate: Swipe left or right with two fingers to flip through webpages, documents, and more—like turning a page in a book.

Open Launchpad: Quickly open apps in Launchpad. Pinch closed with four or five fingers, then click an app to open it.

Swipe between apps: To switch from one full-screen app to another, swipe left or right with three or four fingers.

Customize your gestures. In System Preferences, click Trackpad. You can do the following:

- Learn more about each gesture
- Set the click pressure you prefer to use

- Decide whether to use pressure-sensing features
- Customize other trackpad features

Tip: If you find you're force clicking when you don't intend to, try adjusting the click pressure to a firmer setting in Trackpad preferences. Or change the "Look up & data detectors" option from the "Force Click with one finger" default setting to "Tap with three fingers."

Charge the MacBook Air battery

The battery in your MacBook Air recharges whenever the MacBook Air is connected to power.

Charge the battery. Connect your MacBook Air to a power outlet using the included USB-C Charge Cable and 30W USB-C Power Adapter.

You can charge your MacBook Air using either of the Thunderbolt 3 ports on your computer. The battery charges more quickly when the computer is off or in sleep.

Check the battery's charge. Look at the battery status icon at the right of the menu bar to see the battery level or charging status.

Charging   Charged

Conserve battery power. To extend battery life on a given charge, you can reduce the display brightness, close apps, and disconnect peripheral devices you're not using. Click Energy Saver in System Preferences to change your power settings. If your MacBook Air is in sleep when a device is connected to it, the device's battery may drain.

MacBook Air accessories

The following Apple accessories are available to connect your MacBook Air to power, external devices and displays, and more.

Cable or Adapter	Description
	**USB-C to USB Adapter:** Connect your MacBook Air to standard USB accessories.
	**USB-C to Lightning Cable:** Connect your iPhone or other iOS or iPadOS device to your MacBook Air for syncing and charging.

Cable or Adapter	Description
	**USB-C Digital AV Multiport Adapter:** Connect your MacBook Air to an HDMI display, while also connecting a standard USB device and a USB-C charge cable to charge your MacBook Air.
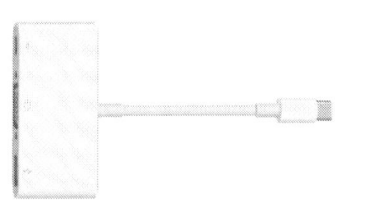	**USB-C VGA Multiport Adapter:** Connect your MacBook Air to a VGA projector or display, while also connecting a standard USB device and a USB-C charge cable to charge your MacBook Air.
	**Thunderbolt 3 (USB-C) to Thunderbolt 2 Adapter:** Connect your MacBook Air to Thunderbolt 2 devices.

For more information about ports and accessories, see the Apple Support article.

Work with wireless accessories

Using Bluetooth® technology, your MacBook Air can wirelessly connect (that is, pair) with devices such as a Bluetooth keyboard, mouse, trackpad, headset, wearable sport accessories, and more.

Connect a Bluetooth device. Turn on the device so that it's discoverable, then open System Preferences and click Bluetooth. Select the device in the list, then click Connect. The device remains connected until you remove it. Control-click a device name to remove it.

Turn Bluetooth on or off. Click the Bluetooth icon ✱ in the menu bar, then choose Turn Bluetooth On or Turn Bluetooth Off. Your MacBook Air comes with Bluetooth turned on.

Tip: If you don't see the Bluetooth icon ✱ in the menu bar, you can add it. Open System Preferences, click Bluetooth, then select "Show Bluetooth in menu bar."

Use an external display with your MacBook Air

The USB-C ports on your MacBook Air support video output. You can use an external display, a projector, or an HDTV with your MacBook Air.

- *Connect a VGA display or projector:* Use a USB-C VGA Multiport Adapter to connect the display to a Thunderbolt 3 (USB-C) port on your MacBook Air.

- *Connect an HDMI display or HDTV:* Use a USB-C Digital AV Multiport Adapter to connect the HDMI display or HDTV to a Thunderbolt 3 (USB-C) port on your MacBook Air.

- *Connect a USB-C display:* Connect the display to a a Thunderbolt 3 (USB-C) port on your MacBook Air.

Adapters and other accessories are sold separately. Visit apple.com, your local Apple Store, or other resellers for more information and availability. Review the documentation or check with the manufacturer to make sure you choose the right product.

Tip: If you have an HDTV connected to an Apple TV, you can use AirPlay to mirror your MacBook Air screen on your TV screen in up to 1080p HD.

Chapter 2
How to Get Started
Set up your Mac

The first time your MacBook Air starts up, Setup Assistant walks you through the simple steps needed to start using your new Mac.

Tip: To use Voice Over during setup, sit idle until you hear the voice command prompting you for a response.

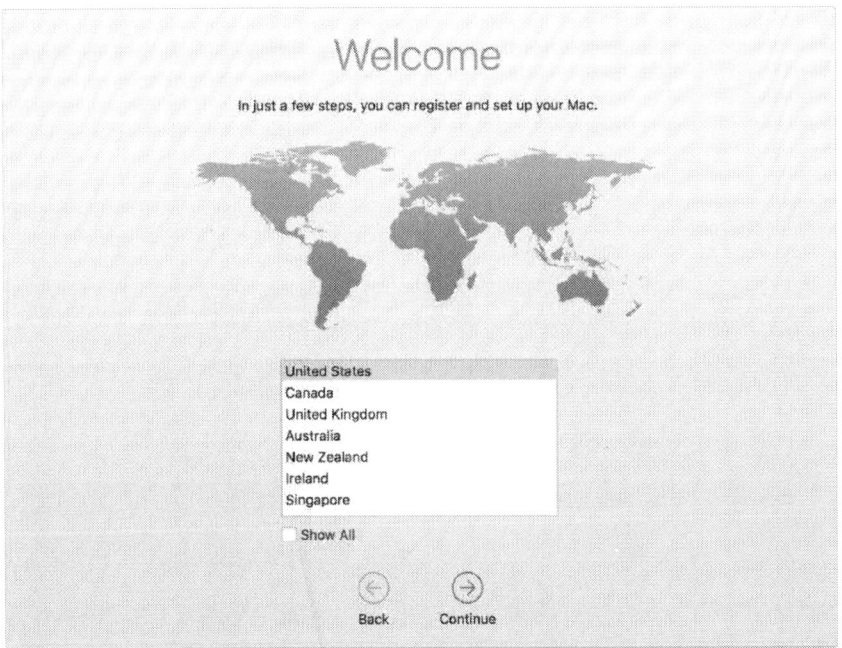

Choose a country to set the language and time zone for your Mac. You can respond to all the prompts, or skip some and choose "Set up later" when you see that option. For example, it might make sense to set up Apple Pay—which requires a verified credit card—and Screen Time—which you can set for different users—after initial setup. Read on for more information about setup tasks.

- *Connect to a Wi-Fi network:* Choose the network and enter a password, if necessary. You can also choose Other Network Options if you're using Ethernet. To change this later, click the Wi-Fi status icon 📶 in the menu bar, then choose a Wi-Fi network and enter the password. You can also choose to Turn Wi-Fi On or Turn Wi-Fi Off here.

  Tip: After setup, if you don't see the Wi-Fi status icon 📶 in the menu bar, you can add it. Open System Preferences, then click Network. Click Wi-Fi in the list on the left, then select "Show Wi-Fi status in menu bar."

- *Transfer information:* If you're setting up a new computer, click "Don't transfer any information now."

- *Sign in with your Apple ID:* Your Apple ID is the account you use for everything you do with Apple—including using the App Store, Apple TV app, Apple Book Store, iCloud, Messages, and more. Your Apple ID consists of an email address and a password. Sign in with the same Apple ID to use any Apple service, on any device—whether it's your computer, iOS device, iPadOS device, or Apple Watch. It's best to have your own Apple ID and not share it. If you don't already have an Apple ID, you can create one during setup (it's free).

If other family members use Apple devices, make sure that each family member has their own Apple ID. You can create Apple ID accounts for your kids and share purchases and subscriptions with Family Sharing.

Important: If you forget your Apple ID password, you don't need to create a new Apple ID. Just click the "Forgot Apple ID or password?" link in the sign in window to retrieve your password.

- *Screen Time:* Monitor and get reports on the use of your computer.

- *Enable Siri and "Hey Siri":* You can turn on Siri and "Hey Siri" (so you can speak your Siri requests) during setup. To enable "Hey Siri," speak several Siri commands when prompted.

- *Store files in iCloud:* With iCloud, you can store all of your content—documents, movies, music, photos, and more—in the cloud, and access it anywhere you go. Be sure to sign in with the same Apple ID on all your devices. To set this option later, open System Preferences and sign in with your Apple ID if you haven't already. Click Apple ID > iCloud, then select the features you want to use.

- *Choose an appearance:* Select Light, Dark, or Auto for your desktop appearance. If you want to change the choice you make during setup, open System Preferences, click General, then select an appearance option. You can also set other preferences here.

- *Set up Touch ID:* You can add a fingerprint to Touch ID during setup. To set up Touch ID later, or to add additional fingerprints, open System Preferences, then click Touch ID. To add a fingerprint, click $+$ and follow the onscreen instructions.

    You can also set options for how you want to use Touch ID on your MacBook Air: to unlock your Mac, use Apple Pay, (purchase items on the App Store, Apple TV app, Apple Book Store, and websites, and auto-fill your password.

    Tip: If two or more users use the same MacBook Air, each user can add a fingerprint to Touch ID to quickly unlock, authenticate, and log in to the MacBook Air. You can add up to three fingerprints per user account, and a total of five fingerprints for all your MacBook Air user accounts.

- *Set up Apple Pay:* You can set up Apple Pay for one user account on your MacBook Air during setup. Other users can still pay with Apple Pay, but they must complete the purchase using their iPhone or Apple Watch that's been set up for Apple Pay. Follow the onscreen prompts to add and verify your card. If you already use a card for media purchases, you might be prompted to verify this card first.

To set up Apple Pay or add additional cards later, open System Preferences, then click Wallet & Apple Pay. Follow the onscreen prompts to set up Apple Pay.

Note: The card issuer determines whether your card is eligible to use with Apple Pay, and may ask you to provide additional information to complete the verification process. Many credit and debit cards can be used with Apple Pay.

Apple Account on Mac

Your Apple ID is an account that lets you access all Apple services. Use your Apple ID to download apps from the App Store; access media in Apple Music, Apple Podcasts, Apple TV, and Apple Books; keep your content up-to-date across devices using iCloud; set up a Family Sharing group; and more. You can also use your Apple ID to access other apps and websites with Sign in with Apple.

All in one place. Manage everything related to your Apple ID in the same place. Open System Preferences on your

MacBook Air—your Apple ID and Family Sharing settings are at the top.

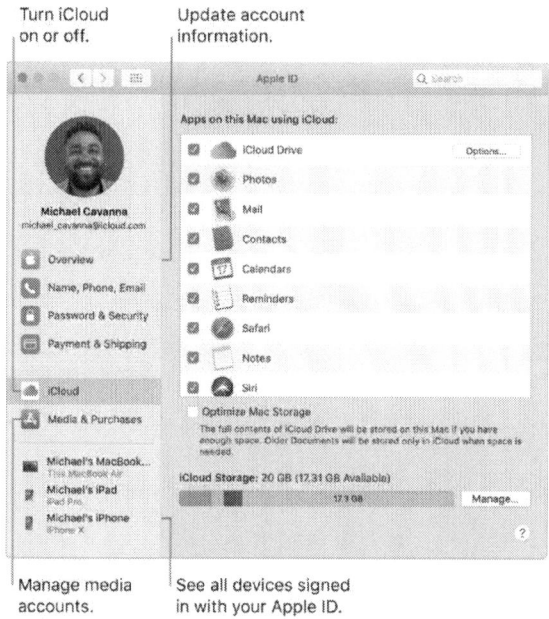

Update account, security, and payment information. In System Preferences, click Apple ID, then select an item in the sidebar to review and update the information associated with your account.

- *Overview:* The Overview pane lets you know if your account is set up and working properly—if not, you see tips and notifications here.

- *Name, Phone, Email:* Update the name and contact information associated with your Apple ID. You can also manage Apple email newsletter subscriptions.

21

- *Password & Security:* Change your Apple ID password, turn on two-factor authentication, add or remove trusted phone numbers, and generate verification codes to sign in to another device or iCloud.com. You can also manage which apps and websites use Sign in with Apple.

- *Payment & Shipping:* Manage the payment methods affiliated with your Apple ID, and your shipping address for purchases from the Apple Store.

- *iCloud:* Select the checkbox next to any iCloud feature to turn it on. When you turn on an iCloud feature, your content is stored in iCloud and not locally on your Mac, so you can access it on any device with iCloud turned on.

- *Media & Purchases:* Manage the accounts linked to Apple Music, Apple Podcasts, Apple TV, and Apple Books; select purchasing settings; and manage your subscriptions.

See all your devices. At the bottom of the Apple ID sidebar, see all the devices linked to your Apple ID. You can verify that Find My [*device*] is turned on for each one, see the status of iCloud Backup for an iOS or iPadOS device, or remove a device from your account if you no longer own it.

Family Sharing. With Family Sharing, you can set up a family group and create Apple ID accounts for your kids. To manage your family sharing settings, click Family Sharing in System

Preferences and select an icon in the sidebar to review and update your information.

The desktop, menu bar, and Help on your Mac

The first thing you see on your MacBook Air is the *desktop*, where you can quickly open apps, search for anything on your MacBook Air and the web, organize your files, and more.

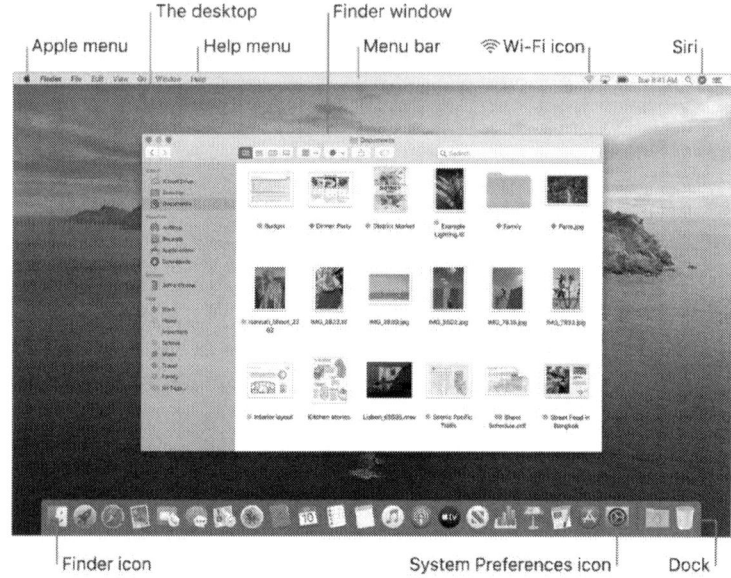

Tip: Can't find the pointer? To magnify it temporarily, move your finger rapidly back and forth on the trackpad. Or if you're using a mouse, slide it back and forth quickly.

Menu bar. Use the menus and icons along the top of the screen to open new windows, connect to a Wi-Fi network, check your Wi-Fi status, change the volume, check your battery charge 🔋, query Siri, and more. The menu items change, depending on which app you're using.

Apple menu . The Apple menu in the upper-left corner of the screen contains frequently used items. To open it, click the Apple icon .

Help menu. Help for your MacBook Air and macOS apps is always available from the Finder. To get help, click the Help menu and choose macOS Help to open the macOS User Guide. Or type in the search field and choose a suggestion.

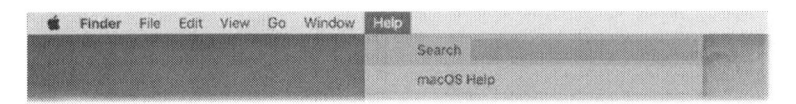

Stay organized with stacks. To create stacks on your desktop, go to Finder and choose View, then select Use Stacks. To see options for your stacks, go to View > Group Stacks By. Then any new files you add to the desktop are automatically sorted into the appropriate stack. To view what's inside a stack, click the stack to expand its contents. You can also place your cursor over a stack to view file thumbnails.

The Finder on your Mac

Use the Finder to organize and locate your files. To open a Finder window, click the Finder icon in the Dock at the bottom of the screen. Force click a file icon to quickly view its contents, or force click a filename to edit it.

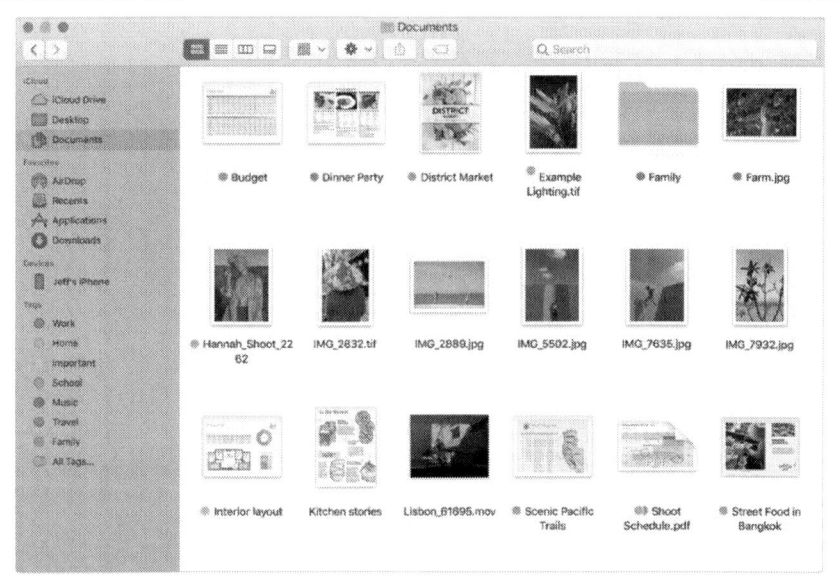

Sync devices. When you connect a device like an iPhone or iPad, you can see it in the Finder sidebar. From there you can back up, update, and restore your device.

Gallery View. With Gallery View, you can see a large preview of a selected file, which gives you a quick way to visually identify images, video clips, and other documents. The Preview pane shows information to help you identify the file you want. Use the scrubber bar at the bottom to quickly locate what you're looking for. To close or open the Preview pane, press Shift-Command-P.

Tip: To show filenames in Gallery View, press Command-J and select "Show filename."

Gallery View

Scrubber bar

Quick Actions. At the bottom right of the Preview pane are shortcuts that let you manage and edit files right in the Finder. You can rotate an image, annotate or crop an image in Markup, combine images and PDFs into a single file, trim audio and video files, and create custom actions through Automator workflows (for example, watermarking a file).

To show the Preview pane options in the Finder, choose View > Show Preview. To customize what's shown, choose View > Show Preview Options, then select the options for your file type.

Tip: Select a file and press the Space bar to open Quick Look. You can sign PDFs; trim audio and video files; and mark up, rotate, and crop images without opening a separate app.

The Dock on your Mac

The Dock, at the bottom of the screen, is a convenient place to keep the apps and documents you use frequently.

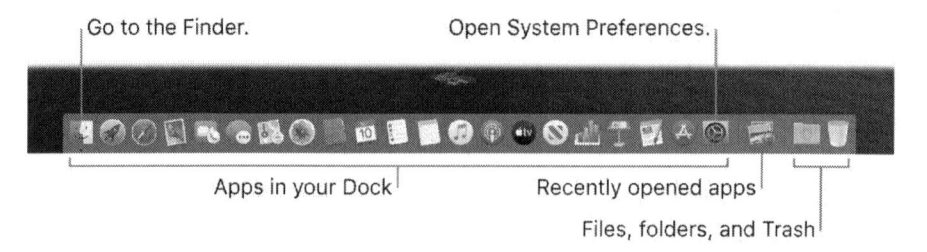

Go to the Finder. *Open System Preferences.*
Apps in your Dock *Recently opened apps*
Files, folders, and Trash

Open an app or file. Click its icon in the Dock. Recently opened apps appear in the center section of the Dock.

Add an item to the Dock. Drag the item and drop it where you want it. Place apps in the left section of the Dock, and files or folders in the right section.

Remove an item from the Dock. Drag it out of the Dock. The item isn't removed from your MacBook Air—just from the Dock.

See all open windows in an app. Force click an app in the Dock to access Exposé and view all the app's open windows.

Tip: Click Dock in System Preferences to make the Dock larger or smaller, add or remove items, move it to the left or right side of the screen, and even set it to hide when you're not using it.

Notification Center on your Mac

Use Notification Center to view details about your day (calendar, stocks, weather, and more) and catch up on notifications you might have missed (email, reminders, app notifications, and more).

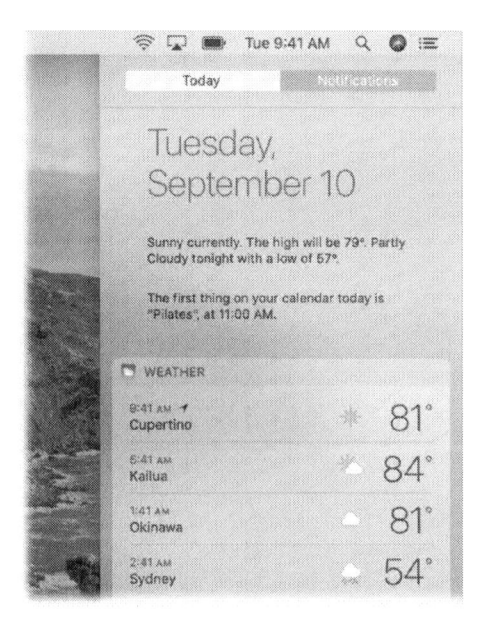

Open Notification Center. Click the Notification Center icon ☰ at the top right of the screen. Click Today to see what's coming up, or Notifications to review what's come in.

Silence notifications. Open Notification Center, scroll up, then turn on Do Not Disturb. You won't see or hear notifications as they arrive, but you can view them later in Notification Center.

System Preferences on your Mac

System Preferences is the place where you personalize your MacBook Air settings. For example, use Energy Saver preferences to change sleep settings. Or use Desktop & Screen

Saver preferences to add a desktop picture or choose a screen saver.

Customize your MacBook Air. Click the System Preferences icon ⚙ in the Dock, or choose Apple menu > System Preferences. Then click the type of preference you want to set.

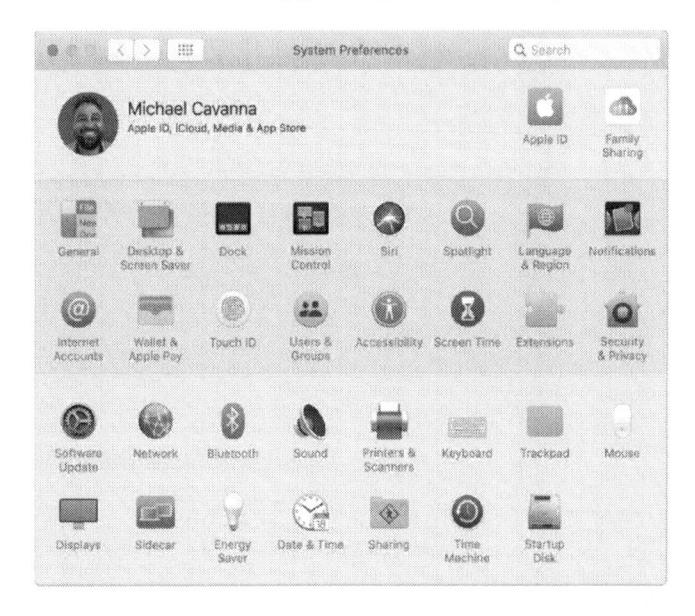

Update macOS. In System Preferences, click Software Update to see if your Mac is running the latest version of macOS software. You can specify options for automatic software updates.

Spotlight on your Mac

Spotlight 🔍 is an easy way to find anything on your MacBook Air, such as documents, contacts, calendar events, and email messages. Spotlight Suggestions offer info from Wikipedia

29

articles, web search results, news, sports, weather, stocks, movies, and other sources.

When you search with Spotlight, the preview area on the right provides search results you can interact with—make a call, send an email message, play a song, get directions, even convert currencies. Spotlight can provide answers to math questions or define words, all on your desktop.

Search for anything. Click 🔍 at the top right of the screen, then start typing.

Tip: Type Command–Space bar to show or hide the Spotlight search field.

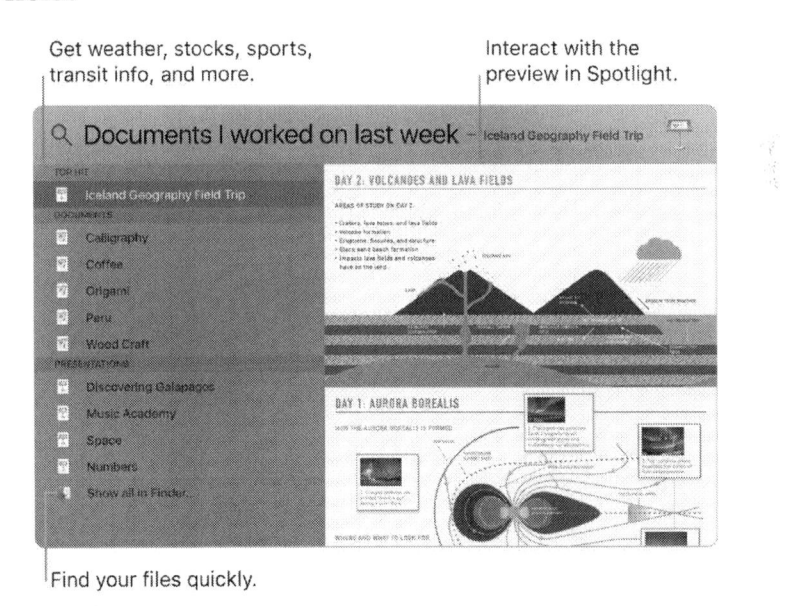

Get weather, stocks, sports, transit info, and more.

Interact with the preview in Spotlight.

Find your files quickly.

Get flight info. Enter the airline and flight number in Spotlight to see your flight status and a map, without having to open Safari.

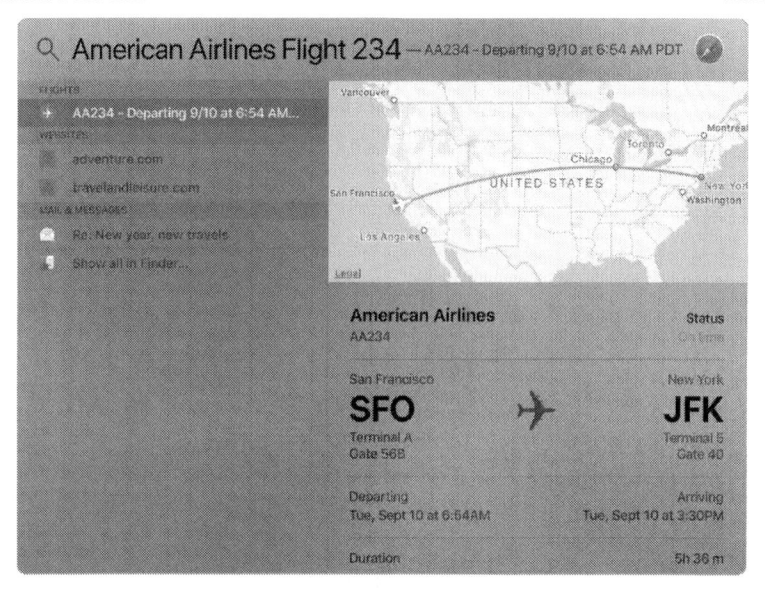

Preview your results. Click a search result and view it in the preview on the right. Sometimes that's all you need to do—click items or links directly in the preview. You can also double-click a result to open it.

Open an app. Type the app name in Spotlight, then press Return.

Turn off Spotlight Suggestions. If you want Spotlight to search only for items on your MacBook Air, you can turn off Spotlight Suggestions in Spotlight preferences. Open System Preferences, click Spotlight, then click to deselect "Allow Spotlight Suggestions in Look up." Make any other changes you want to the list of categories Spotlight searches.

Siri on your Mac

You can talk to Siri on your MacBook Air and use your voice for many tasks. For example, you can find files, schedule meetings, change preferences, get answers, send messages, place calls, and add items to your calendar. Siri can give you directions ("How do I get home from here?"), provide information ("How high is Mount Whitney?"), perform basic tasks ("Create a new grocery list"), and much more.

On your MacBook Air, Siri is available whenever you say "Hey Siri" and immediately speak your request (your MacBook Air lid must be open). Play music, set up a meeting, open a file, and more by using your voice. You can enable the "Listen for 'Hey Siri'" option in the Siri pane of System Preferences.

Note: Siri may not be available in all languages or in all areas, and features may vary by area.

Enable Siri. Click the Siri icon in the menu bar, then click Enable when prompted. If you enabled Siri during setup, clicking the icon opens Siri. Or click Siri in System Preferences, then select Enable Ask Siri. You can set other preferences in the Siri pane, such as Language and whether to show Siri in the menu bar.

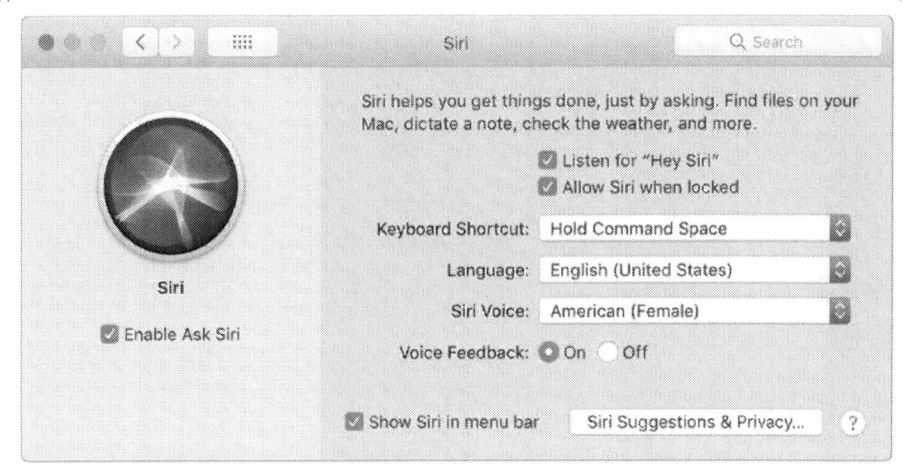

Note: To use Siri, your MacBook Air must be connected to the internet.

Speak to Siri. Click Siri in the menu bar and start speaking. Or press and hold the Command key and the Space bar, and speak to Siri.

Hey Siri. On your MacBook Air, you can simply say "Hey Siri" to get responses to your requests. To enable this feature in the Siri pane of System Preferences, click "Listen for 'Hey Siri'," then speak several Siri commands when prompted.

For convenience, "Hey Siri" doesn't respond when the lid to your MacBook Air is closed. If the lid is closed *and* connected to an external display, you can still invoke Siri from the icon in the menu bar.

Tip: To learn about more ways you can use Siri, ask "What can you do?" at any time, or click the Help button .

Some things you can ask me:

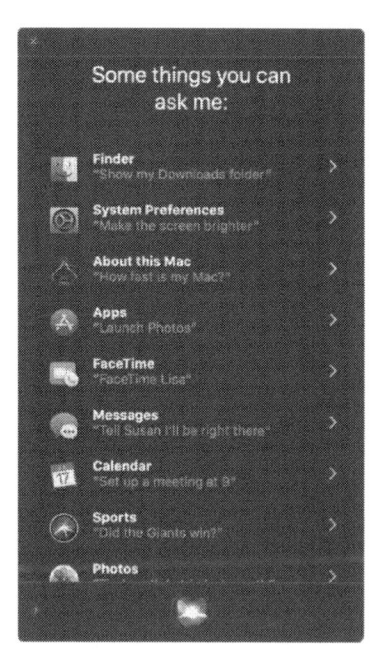

- **Finder** — "Show my Downloads folder"
- **System Preferences** — "Make the screen brighter"
- **About this Mac** — "How fast is my Mac?"
- **Apps** — "Launch Photos"
- **FaceTime** — "FaceTime Lisa"
- **Messages** — "Tell Susan I'll be right there"
- **Calendar** — "Set up a meeting at 9"
- **Sports** — "Did the Giants win?"
- **Photos**

Play some music. Just say, "Play some music," and Siri does the rest. You can even tell Siri, "Play the top song from March 1991."

Find and open files. Ask Siri to find files and open them right from the Siri window. You can ask by filename or by description. For example, "Show me files Ursula sent," or "Open the spreadsheet I created last night."

Drag and drop. Drag and drop images and locations from the Siri window into an email, text message, or document. You can also copy and paste text.

Pin a result. Save Siri results from sporting events, Reminders, Clock, Stocks, Notes, Finder, and general knowledge (Wikipedia, for example) to the Today view in Notifications.

Click the plus sign ⊕ in the top right of a Siri result to pin it to the Today view. To see it later, click the Notification Center icon ☰, then click Today. If you're checking a sports score, for example, results stay up to date.

Change the voice. Click Siri in System Preferences, then choose an option from the Siri Voice menu.

Throughout this guide, you'll find suggestions for things you can ask Siri—they look like this:

Ask Siri. Say something like:

- "Open the Keynote presentation I was working on last night"
- "What time is it in Paris?"

Quickly open apps on your Mac

- Your MacBook Air comes with apps for all the things you love to do—browse the web, check email, share photos, enjoy movies, and more.

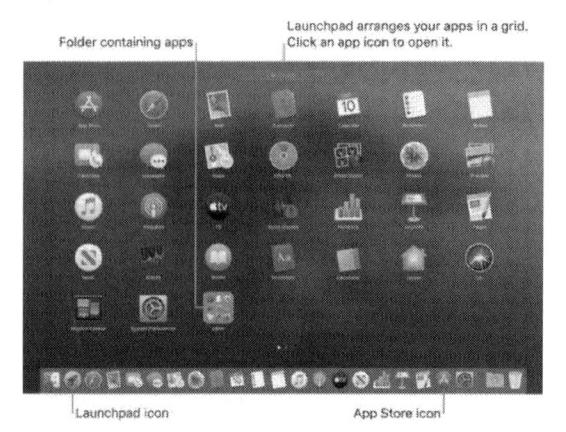

-

- **Open an app.** Click an app icon in the Dock, or click the Launchpad icon in the Dock and click the app you want. You can also search for an app using Spotlight, then open the app directly from your Spotlight search results.
- **Ask Siri.** Say something like: "Open Calculator."
- **Organize apps in Launchpad.** Launchpad organizes your apps in a grid. Drag an app to a new location to rearrange apps. Drag an app onto another app to create a folder. Drag more apps to the new folder to add them. To remove an app from a folder, drag it out.
- **Get more apps.** Click the App Store icon in the Dock and search for apps you want. Apps you download from the App Store appear automatically in Launchpad. To quickly get updates for apps, click Updates in the App Store.

Display settings for your Mac

- **Match the light in your surroundings.** Your MacBook Air has a Retina display with True Tone capability. True Tone technology automatically adapts the color of your display to match the light in your environment for a more natural viewing experience. Turn True Tone on or off in the Displays pane of System Preferences.

- **Use a dynamic desktop.** When you use a dynamic desktop picture, the desktop picture automatically changes to match the time of day in your current location. Click Desktop & Screen Saver in System Preferences, click Desktop, then choose a picture for Dynamic Desktop. To have your screen change based on your current time zone, enable Location Services. If Location Services is turned off, the picture changes based on the time zone specified in Date & Time preferences.
- **Stay focused with Dark Mode.** You can use a dark color scheme for the desktop, menu bar, Dock, and all the built-in macOS apps. Your content stands out front and center while darkened controls and windows recede into the background. See white text on a black background in apps such as Mail, Contacts, Calendar, and Messages, so it's easier on your eyes when you're working in dark environments.

- Dark Mode is finely tuned for professionals who edit photos and images—colors and fine details pop against the dark app backgrounds. But it's also great for anyone who just wants to focus on their content.

  Transfer your data to your new MacBook Air
- It's easy to move your files and settings from another Mac or PC to your MacBook Air. You can transfer information to your MacBook Air from an old computer—or from a Time Machine backup on a USB storage device—either wirelessly, or with an Ethernet cable and adapters.
- **Tip:** For best results, make sure your MacBook Air is running the latest version of macOS. Open System Preferences, then click Software Update to check for updates.
- **Transfer wirelessly.** To transfer the data when you first set up your MacBook Air, use Setup Assistant. To transfer data later, you can use Migration Assistant. Open a Finder window, go to Applications/Utilities, then double-click Migration Assistant to do a wireless migration. Follow the onscreen instructions.

- **Tip:** To transfer the information wirelessly from your old computer to your MacBook Air, make sure both computers are connected to the same network. Keep both computers near each other throughout the migration process.
- If you used Time Machine to back up your files from another Mac to a storage device (such as an external disk), you can copy the files from the device to your MacBook Air.
- **Copy files from a USB storage device.** Connect the storage device to your MacBook Air using a USB-C to USB. Then drag files from your storage device to your MacBook Air.
- **Transfer using Ethernet.** To transfer your data over Ethernet, use an adapter (available separately) to connect the Ethernet cable to your MacBook Air. Connect the other end of the Ethernet cable to your other computer (you might need another adapter, if your computer doesn't have an Ethernet port). Before transferring your data

using Ethernet, make sure your MacBook Air battery is fully charged.

Back up and restore your Mac

To keep your files safe, it's important to back up your MacBook Air regularly. The easiest way to back up is to use Time Machine—which is built into your MacBook Air—with an external storage device connected to your MacBook Air. Time Machine can also back up your Mac contents to supported network volumes. For a list of devices supported by Time Machine,

Files in iCloud Drive and photos in iCloud Photos are automatically stored in iCloud and don't need to be part of your backup. However, if you'd like them to be, do the following:

- *iCloud Drive:* Open System Preferences, click Apple ID, then click iCloud and deselect Optimize Mac Storage. The contents of your iCloud Drive will be stored on your Mac and included in your backup.

- *iCloud Photos:* Open Photos, then choose Photos > Preferences. In the iCloud pane, select "Download Originals to this Mac." Full-resolution versions of your entire photo library will be stored on your Mac and included in your backup.

Tip: You can use a shared Mac that's on the same network as your MacBook Air as a backup destination. On the other Mac, go to the Sharing pane of System Preferences, then turn on File Sharing. Add a shared folder, secondary click (that is, right-click) the folder, choose Advanced Options, then click "Share as Time Machine backup destination."

Set up Time Machine. Make sure your MacBook Air is on the same Wi-Fi network as your external storage device, or connect your external storage device to your MacBook Air. Open System Preferences, click Time Machine, then select Back Up Automatically. Select the drive you want to use for backup, and you're all set.

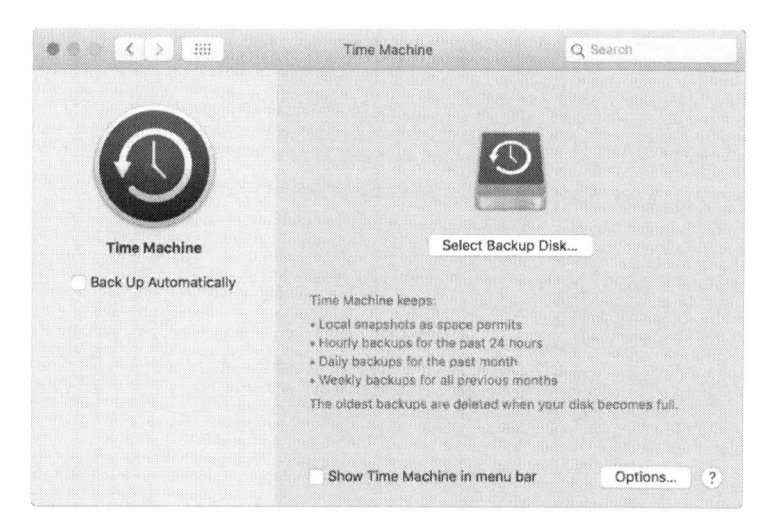

Time Machine:

- Automatically backs up everything on your MacBook Air, including system files, apps, accounts, preferences, music, photos, movies, and documents.

- Remembers how everything looked on any given day, so you can revisit your MacBook Air as it appeared in the past or retrieve an older version of a document.

- Lets you restore your MacBook Air from a Time Machine backup. So if anything happens to your MacBook Air, your files and settings are safe and sound.

Chapter 3
Use MacBook Air with other Devices

Access your iCloud content on your Mac

- iCloud is the easiest way to make sure all your important content is everywhere you are. iCloud stores your documents, photos, music, apps, contacts, and calendars, so you can access them anytime you're connected to the web.
- You can use your Apple ID to set up a free iCloud account, which comes with 5 GB of free storage space. Purchases you make from the iTunes Store, App Store, Apple TV app, or Book Store don't count toward your available space.
- iCloud keeps everything up to date on your devices. So if you have an iPhone, iPad, or iPod touch, just sign in to each device using the same Apple ID, turn on iCloud, and you'll have everything you need.

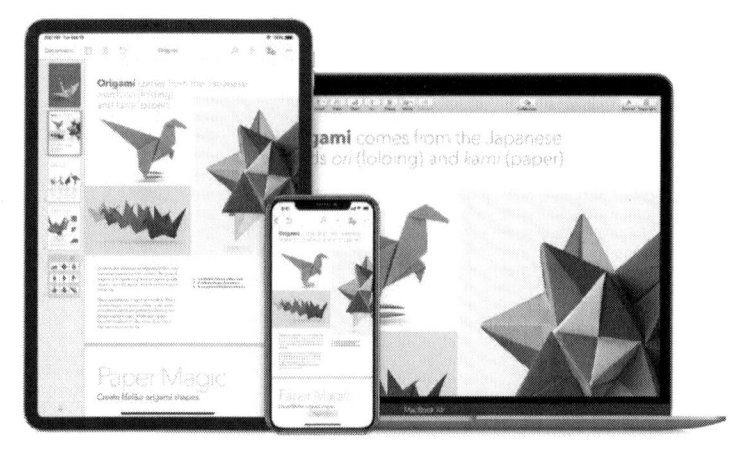

- Here are some of the things you can do with iCloud.
- **Automatically store your desktop and Documents folder in iCloud Drive.** You can save files in your Documents folder or on your desktop, and they're automatically available on iCloud Drive and accessible wherever you are. When working with iCloud Drive, you have access to files on your MacBook Air, on your iPhone or iPad in the Files app, on the web at iCloud.com, or on a Windows PC in the iCloud app. When you make changes to a file on a device or on iCloud Drive, you'll see your edits wherever you view the file.
- To get started, open System Preferences, click Apple ID, then click iCloud. Select iCloud Drive, then click Options and select "Desktop & Documents Folders."
- **Share purchases and storage with Family Sharing.** Up to six members of your family can share their purchases from the iTunes Store, App Store, Apple TV app, and Book Store and share the same storage plan—even if they each use their own iCloud account. Pay for family purchases with one credit card, and approve your kids' spending right from your MacBook Air, iOS device, or iPadOS device. Also share photos, a family calendar, reminders, and locations. To set up Family

Sharing if you didn't when you set up your Mac, open System Preferences, click FamilySharing, then click Next.

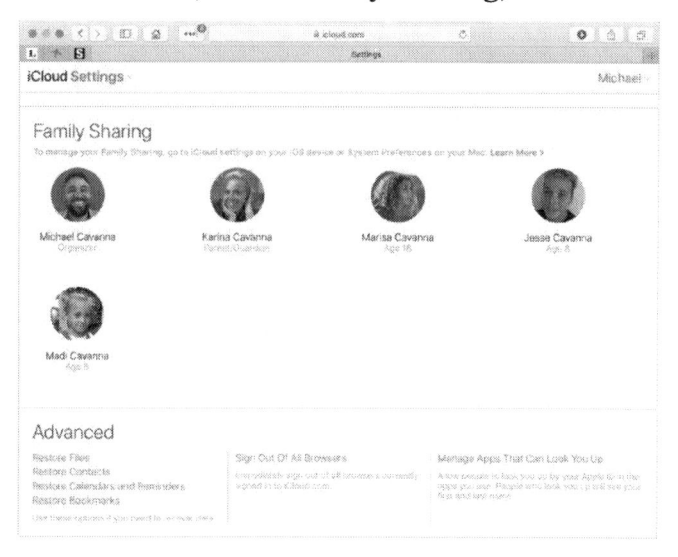

- **Store and share photos using iCloud Photos and Shared Albums.** Store your photo library in iCloud and see your photos and videos, as well as the edits you make to them, on all your devices. Share photos and videos with only the people you choose, and let them add their own photos, videos, and comments. To get started, open System Preferences, click Apple ID > iCloud, select Photos, then click Options.
- **Enjoy your purchases anywhere.** When you're signed in to your devices with the same Apple ID, purchases you've made on the iTunes Store, App Store, Apple TV app, and Book Store are available at any time, no matter which computer or device you used to purchase

them. So all your music, movies, books, and more are available wherever you go.
- **Locate your MacBook Air with Find My Mac.** If your MacBook Air is missing, you can use Find My to locate it on a map, lock its screen, and even erase its data remotely if you have Find My Mac turned on. To turn on Find My Mac, open System Preferences, click Apple ID > iCloud, then select Find My Mac.

  Note: If your MacBook Air has multiple user accounts, only one can have Find My Mac turned on.

Use Handoff on your Mac

- With Handoff, you can continue on one device where you left off on another. Work on a presentation on your MacBook Air, then continue on your iPad. Or start an email message on your iPhone, then finish it on your MacBook Air. View a message on your Apple Watch, and respond to it on your MacBook Air. You don't have to worry about transferring files. When your MacBook Air and devices are near each other, an icon appears in the Dock whenever an activity can be handed off; to continue, just click the icon.
- *Note:* To use Handoff, you need an iPhone, iPad, or iPod touch with the Lightning or USB-C connector and iOS 8 (or later) or iPadOS installed. Make sure your MacBook Air, iOS device, or iPadOS device have Wi-Fi and

Bluetooth turned on and are signed in with the same Apple ID.

- Click to continue what you were doing on your iPhone.

- **Turn on Handoff on your MacBook Air.** Open System Preferences, click General, then select "Allow Handoff between this Mac and your iCloud devices."

- **Turn on Handoff on your iOS or iPadOS device.** Go to Settings > General > Handoff, then tap to turn on Handoff. If you don't see the option, your device doesn't support Handoff.

- **Turn on Handoff on your Apple Watch.** In the Apple Watch app on iPhone, go to Settings > General, then tap to turn on Enable Handoff.

- Handoff works with Safari, Mail, Calendar, Contacts, Maps, Messages, Notes, Reminders, Keynote, Numbers, and Pages.

Use Universal Clipboard on your Mac

- Copy content from one device, and paste it to another nearby device within a short period of time. The contents of your clipboard are sent over Wi-Fi and made available to all Mac, iPhone, iPad, and iPod touch devices that are signed in with the same Apple ID and have Handoff, Wi-Fi, and Bluetooth turned on. See Use Handoff on your Mac.

- *Note:* To use Universal Clipboard, you need an iPhone, iPad, or iPod touch with the Lightning or USB-C connector and iOS 10 (or later) or iPadOS installed.

-

- **Use across apps.** You can copy and paste images, text, photos, and video between any apps that support copy and paste on your Mac, iPhone, iPad, and iPod touch.

- **Copy and paste files.** You can quickly move files from one Mac to another using Universal Clipboard. Copy a file on your MacBook Air and paste it to a Finder window, Mail message, or any app that supports copy and paste on a nearby Mac. You must be signed in with the same Apple ID on both Macs.

Continuity Camera on your Mac

- Use your iPhone, iPad, or iPod touch to scan documents or take a picture of something nearby, and it appears instantly on your Mac. Continuity Camera is supported in many apps, including Finder, Mail, Messages, and more.

- *Note:* To use Continuity Camera, you need an iPhone, iPad, or iPod touch with iOS 12 (or later) or iPadOS installed. Make sure your MacBook Air and iOS or iPadOS device have Wi-Fi and Bluetooth turned on and are signed in with the same Apple ID.

- **Insert an image or scan.** In an app like Mail, Notes, or Messages, select where you want the image to go, choose File (or Insert) > Import From iPhone or iPad, choose "Take Photo" or "Scan Documents," then take the photo or scan the image on your iOS or iPadOS device. You might need to select your iOS or iPadOS device before taking the photo. Tap Use Photo or Keep Scan. You can also tap Retake if you want to try again.

- In an app such as Pages, select where you want the image to be inserted, then secondary click (that is, right-click), choose "Import image," and take the photo. You might need to select your device before taking the photo.

- *Note:* To take a scan on your iOS or iPadOS device, drag the frame until what you want to show is in the frame, tap Keep Scan, then tap Save. Tap Retake to rescan the content.

- The photo or scan appears where you want it in your document.

Continuity Sketch and Continuity Markup on your Mac

With Continuity Sketch, you can use your nearby iPhone or iPad to draw a sketch and instantly insert it into a document on your Mac—for example, in an email, a message, a document, or a note. Or use Continuity Markup to edit a document using your finger on an iOS device or with Apple Pencil on an iPad, and see those markups on your Mac.

Note: To use Continuity Sketch and Continuity Markup, you need an iPhone or iPod touch with iOS 13 or an iPad with iPadOS installed. Make sure your MacBook Air and iOS or iPadOS device have Wi-Fi and Bluetooth turned on and are signed in with the same Apple ID. Pressure and tilt for Apple Pencil only work in apps with advanced stylus support.

Insert a sketch. In an app like Mail, Notes, or Messages, position the cursor where you want to insert a sketch. Choose File (or Insert) > Import from iPhone or iPad, then choose Add Sketch. On your iOS device or iPad, draw a sketch using your finger or Apple Pencil (on an iPad that supports it), then tap Done. On your Mac, the sketch appears where you positioned the cursor. Depending on where the sketch is inserted, you can mark it up or adjust other aspects, such as enlarge the size.

Mark up a document. With Continuity Markup, you can use a nearby iPad, iPhone, or iPod touch to mark up PDFs, screenshots, and images, and see the results on your Mac. Press and hold the Space bar to view the document in Quick Look, then click the iPad Markup icon . Start writing, drawing, or adding shapes with your finger or Apple Pencil (on an iPad that supports it). See the updates live on your Mac as you make them on your iPhone, iPod touch, or iPad.

AirDrop on your Mac

AirDrop makes it easy to share files with nearby Mac, iPhone, iPad, and iPod touch devices. The devices don't need to share the same Apple ID.

Note: AirDrop for iOS or iPadOS requires devices that have the Lightning or USB-C connector and iOS 7 (or later) or iPadOS. Not all older Macs support AirDrop (for a list of supported Macs, see the Apple Support article Use AirDrop on your Mac).

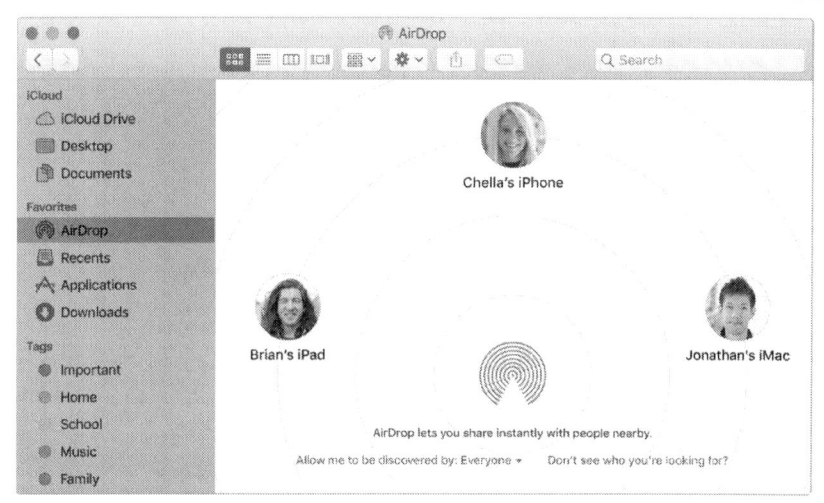

Send a file from the Finder. Click the Finder icon in the Dock, then click AirDrop in the sidebar on the left. When the person you want to send a file to appears in the window, drag the file to him or her.

Send a file from an app. While using an app like Pages or Preview, click the Share button and choose AirDrop.

Share passwords stored in iCloud Keychain. In Safari, you can use AirDrop to share an account password with one of your contacts, or with another Mac, iPhone, iPad, or iPod touch. From the Safari menu, open Preferences > Passwords, select the website whose password you want to share, then secondary click (that is, right-click). Choose "Share with AirDrop," then select the person or device in the AirDrop window to share the password.

Control who can send items to you using AirDrop. Click the Finder icon in the Dock, click AirDrop in the sidebar, then click "Allow me to be discovered by" and choose an option.

When you send a file to someone, the recipient can choose whether or not to accept the file. When someone sends you a file, you can find it in the Downloads folder on your MacBook Air.

Tip: If you don't see the recipient in the AirDrop window, make sure both devices have AirDrop and Bluetooth turned on and are within 30 feet (9 meters) of each other. If the recipient is using an older Mac, try clicking the "Don't see who you're looking for?" link.

Phone calls and text messages on your Mac

You can take calls—and make them—right from your MacBook Air. You can also receive and send text messages.

Note: A Wi-Fi connection is required in order to make or receive phone calls on your MacBook Air.

Take or make a call. When someone calls your iPhone, click the notification that appears on your MacBook Air screen. Your MacBook Air becomes a speakerphone. If you want to make a call, click a phone number in a Spotlight search or in an app such as FaceTime, Contacts, Safari, or Calendar. You need a nearby device (iPhone or iPad) with a cellular connection in order to make phone calls.

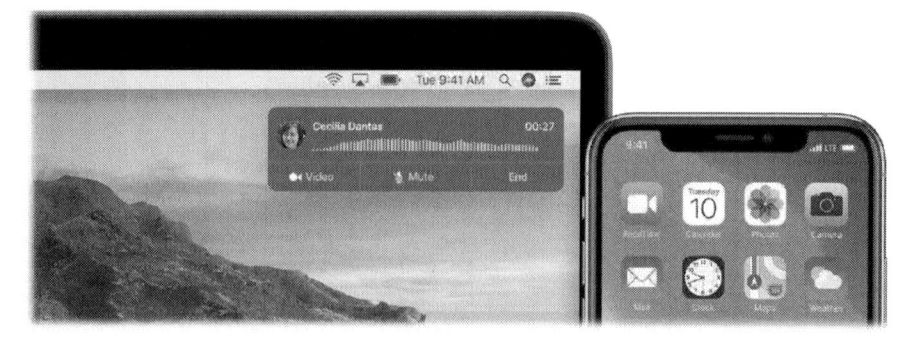

Send and receive messages. Send and receive SMS and MMS text messages right from your MacBook Air. When friends and family text you, you can respond with whichever device is closest.

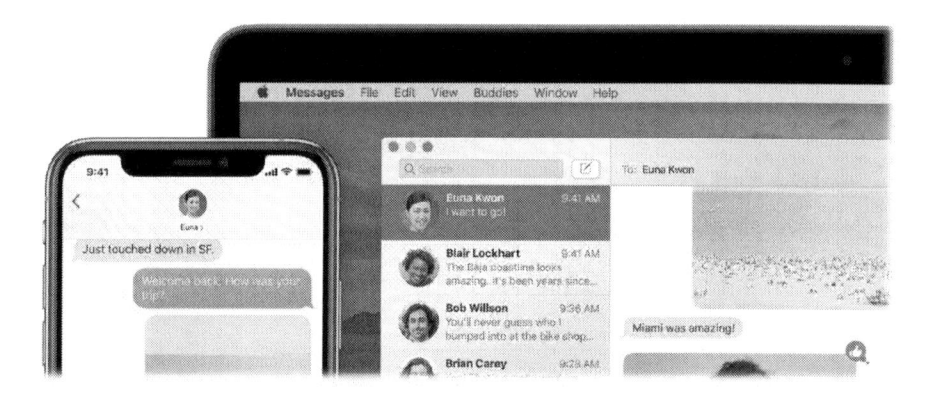

Instant Hotspot on your Mac

Lost your Wi-Fi connection? With Instant Hotspot, you can use the Personal Hotspot on your iPhone or iPad to connect your MacBook Air to the internet instantly—no password required.

Note: Personal Hotspot requires an iPhone or cellular-model iPad, with iOS 8 (or later) or iPadOS.

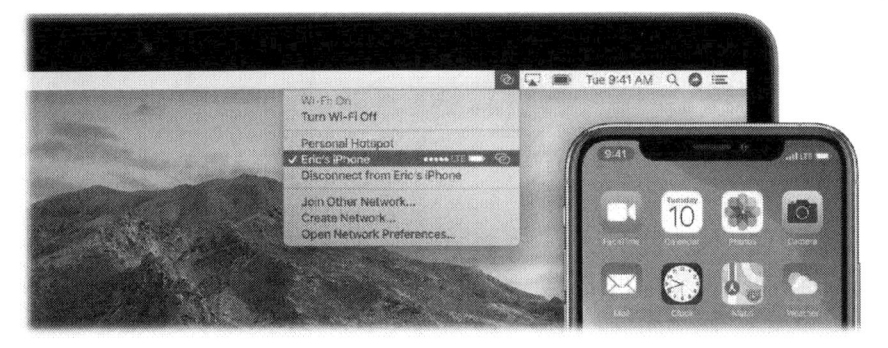

Connect to your device's Personal Hotspot. Click the Wi-Fi status icon 🛜 in the menu bar, then choose your iPhone or iPad from the list of devices that appears. The Wi-Fi icon changes to ⦾. (You don't need to do anything on your device—MacBook Air connects automatically.)

Tip: If you're asked for a password, make sure your devices are set up correctly.

Check the status of your connection. Look in the Wi-Fi status menu to see the strength of the cellular signal.

When you're not using the hotspot, your MacBook Air disconnects to save battery life.

Unlock your Mac and approve tasks with Apple Watch

When you're wearing your Apple Watch, you can use it to automatically unlock your MacBook Air and approve authentication tasks—such as entering passwords, unlocking notes and preferences, and authorizing installations—without having to type a password. These features use strong encryption to provide secure communication between your Apple Watch and MacBook Air.

To use the Auto Unlock and Approve with Apple Watch features:

- Sign in to your Mac and Apple Watch with the same Apple ID.

- Make sure your Apple Watch is unlocked and running watchOS 3 or later to automatically unlock your Mac; approving authentication requests requires watchOS 6 or later.

- Turn on two-factor authentication (see below).

Set up two-factor authentication for your Apple ID. To turn on two-factor authentication, go to Apple menu > System Preferences > Apple ID > Password & Security, then select Set Up Two-Factor Authentication. Make sure "Disable automatic login" is also selected. (You won't see this option if you're using FileVault, but you can still use the Auto Unlock and Approve with Apple Watch features.)

Set up Auto Unlock. Sign in to all your devices with the same Apple ID, then open System Preferences on your MacBook Air. If your Apple Watch has watchOS 6 installed, click Security & Privacy, then click General and select "Use your Apple Watch to unlock apps and your Mac." If your Apple Watch has watchOS 3 to watchOS 5 installed, select "Allow your Apple Watch to unlock your Mac." You can't approve authentication tasks unless you have watchOS 6 or later.

Note: These features work only when your Apple Watch is authenticated with a passcode. You authenticate your Apple Watch each time you put it on, so no extra steps are necessary after you enter your passcode.

Skip the sign-in. Walk up to your sleeping MacBook Air wearing your authenticated Apple Watch on your wrist, and lift the cover or press a key to wake your MacBook Air—Apple Watch unlocks it so you can get right to work.

Approve with Apple Watch. If you're prompted for a password, double-click the side button on your Apple Watch to authenticate your password on your Mac. You can view your passwords in Safari, approve app installations, unlock a locked note, and more (requires watchOS 6).

Use Apple Pay on your Mac

You can make easy, secure, and private purchases on websites using Apple Pay on your MacBook Air. With Apple Pay, your Apple Card and other credit or debit card information is never stored or shared by Apple with the merchant. When you shop online using Safari, look for an Apple Pay button. You can complete a purchase using Touch ID on your MacBook Air. Otherwise, use your iPhone or Apple Watch to complete the purchase. Keep reading for details.

Note: Apple Pay and Apple Card aren't available in all countries or regions.

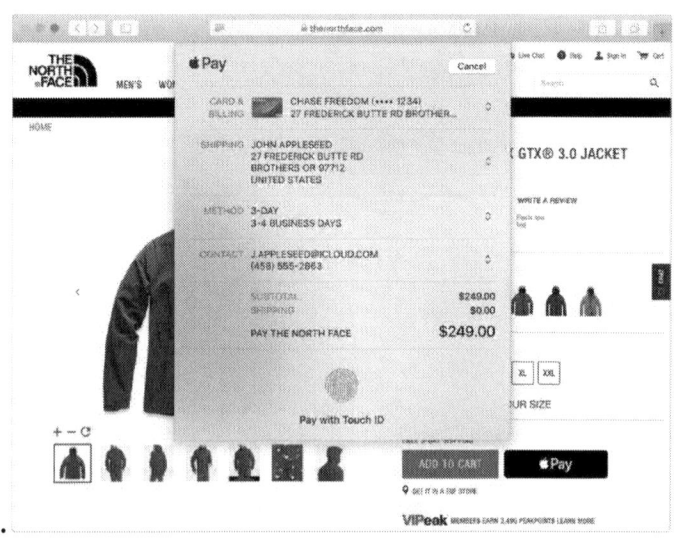

Make a purchase using Touch ID. On your MacBook Air, you're prompted to configure Apple Pay during setup. When you choose Apple Pay on a website, place your finger lightly on the Touch ID sensor to authenticate and complete your purchase.

Make a purchase with iPhone or Apple Watch. You can use your iPhone or Apple Watch to complete a purchase. No extra setup is required—Apple Pay uses the Apple Card or other credit or debit cards you've already set up on your iPhone or Apple Watch. You must be signed in to an iPhone or Apple Watch that has Apple Pay set up with the same Apple ID you're using on your MacBook Air. Click the Apple Pay button on the website, then to confirm the payment, use Face ID, Touch ID, or the passcode on your iPhone, or double-click the side button on your unlocked Apple Watch.

Note: If you don't choose to set up Apple Pay when you first start up your MacBook Air, you can set it up later in the Wallet & Apple Pay pane of System Preferences. Manage your Apple Card and other payment cards there—add or delete cards and make updates to contact information.

Use AirPlay on your Mac

Show whatever's on your MacBook Air on the big screen using AirPlay Mirroring. To mirror the MacBook Air screen on your TV screen or to use the HDTV as a second display, connect your HDTV to Apple TV and make sure the Apple TV is on the same Wi-Fi network as your MacBook Air. You can also play web videos directly on your HDTV without showing what's on your desktop—handy when you want to play a movie but keep your work private.

Mirror your desktop using AirPlay Mirroring. Click the AirPlay icon ![icon] in the menu bar, then choose your Apple TV. When an AirPlay display is active, the icon turns blue.

In some cases, you can use an AirPlay display even if your MacBook Air isn't on the same Wi-Fi network as Apple TV (called *peer-to-peer AirPlay*). To use peer-to-peer AirPlay, you need an Apple TV (3rd generation rev A, model A1469 or later) with Apple TV software 7.0 or later.

Play web videos without showing your desktop. When you find a web video with an AirPlay icon ![icon], click the icon, then select your Apple TV.

Tip: If the image doesn't fit your HDTV screen when you mirror the screen, adjust the desktop size for the best picture. Click the AirPlay icon, then choose an option under "Match Desktop Size To."

Apple TV is sold separately at apple.com or your local Apple Store.

Use AirPrint on your Mac

You can use AirPrint to print wirelessly to:

- An AirPrint-enabled printer on your Wi-Fi network
- A network printer or printer shared by another Mac on your Wi-Fi network
- A printer connected to the USB port of an AirPort base station

Print to an AirPrint printer. When you print from an app, click the Printer pop-up menu in the Print dialog, then choose a printer in the Nearby Printers list.

Can't find the printer you're looking for? Make sure it's connected to the same Wi-Fi network as your MacBook Air. If it's connected and you still don't see it, try adding it: open System Preferences, click Printers & Scanners, then click +. (You may have to temporarily connect the printer to your MacBook Air using a USB cable and, if necessary, an adapter.)

Chapter 4

Apps included with your Mac

Your MacBook Air comes with a collection of great apps for things you do every day, like surfing the web, sending mail and messages, and arranging your calendar. It also comes with apps like Photos, Apple Music, Apple Podcasts, the Apple TV app, Pages, Numbers, and Keynote—so you can be creative and productive right from the start. The apps that come with your MacBook Air are described in the following sections.

Note: Some macOS apps are not available in every region or language.

Find even more apps. Click the App Store icon in the Dock to find apps for everything you want to do.

App Store

Search the App Store to find and download apps, and get the latest updates for your apps.

Find the perfect app. Know exactly what you're looking for? Type the name in the search field, then press Return.

Note: Apple Arcade is not available in all countries or regions.

Ask Siri. Say something like: "Find apps for kids."

All you need is an Apple ID. To download apps, sign in with your Apple ID—choose Store > Sign In, or click Sign In at the bottom of the sidebar. If you don't have an Apple ID yet, click

Sign In, then click Create Apple ID. If you have an Apple ID but don't remember your password, click Forgot to recover it.

Get the latest updates. If you see a badge on the App Store icon in the Dock, there are updates available. Click the icon to open the App Store, then click Updates in the sidebar.

Tip: You can spread the word about your favorite apps to your friends. While viewing an app, click the down arrow next to the price, then choose Tell a Friend.

Books

Use Apple Books to read and organize your library of books and audio books, and to purchase new books on your Mac.

Note: Apple Books is not available in all countries or regions.

A bookshelf on your Mac. Browse or search all the items in your library—or click Book Store to find new books and other publications. To buy an item, just sign in with your Apple ID (choose Store > Sign in). **Ask Siri.** Say something like: "Find books by Jane Austen."

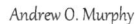

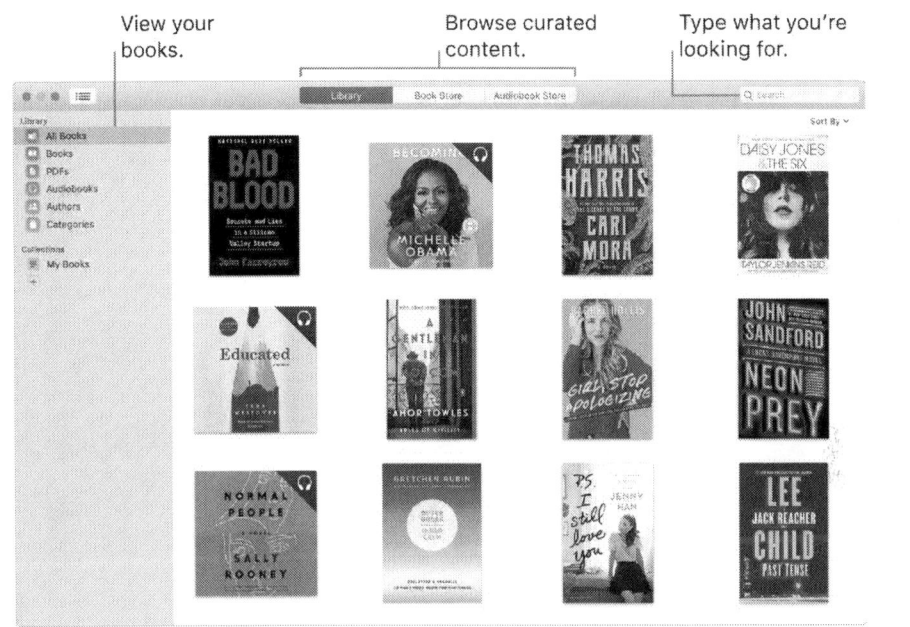

Never lose your place or your markups. Your purchased books, collections, highlights, notes, bookmarks, and the current page you're reading are available automatically on your Mac, iOS devices, and iPadOS devices, as long as you're signed in on them with the same Apple ID.

Find your way back. You can quickly go to pages you've bookmarked. Click the arrow next to ▌ to view your list of bookmarks.

Tip: Change to Night theme to read more easily in low-light situations. Choose View > Theme, then choose Night, or click the Appearance button A, then click the black circle. Not all books support Night theme.

Calendar

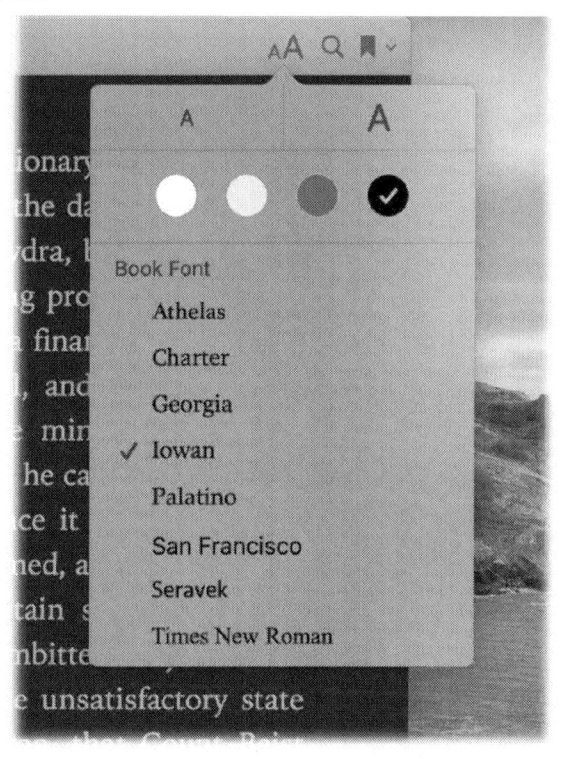

Never miss an appointment with Calendar. Keep track of your busy schedule by creating multiple calendars, and manage them all in one place.

Create events. Click + to add a new event, or double-click anywhere in a day. To invite someone, double-click the event, click the Add Invitees section, then type an email address. Calendar lets you know when your invitees reply.

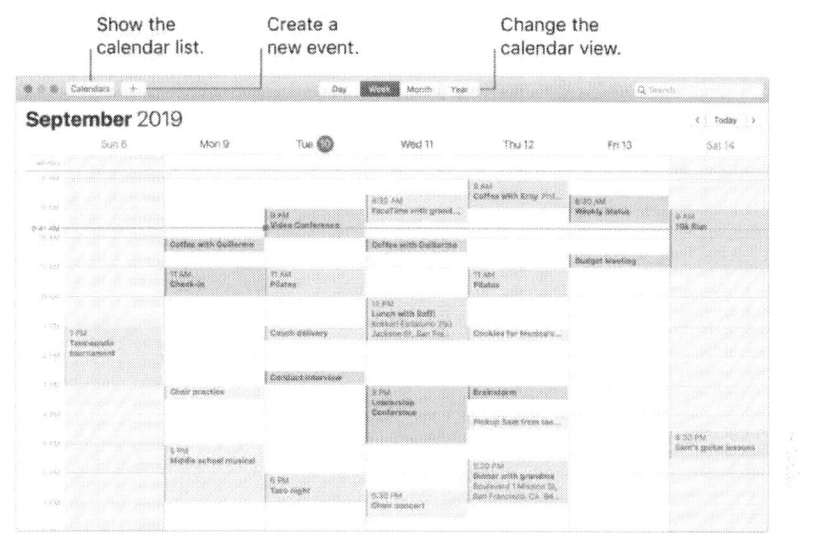

See all your calendars—or just a few. Click the Calendars button to see a list of all your calendars; click the ones you want to see in the window.

Ask Siri. Say something like: "Set up a meeting with Mark at nine in the morning."

A calendar for every part of your life. Create separate calendars—for example, for home, work, and school—each with its own color. Choose File > New Calendar to create a calendar, then secondary click (that is, right-click) each calendar to choose a new color.

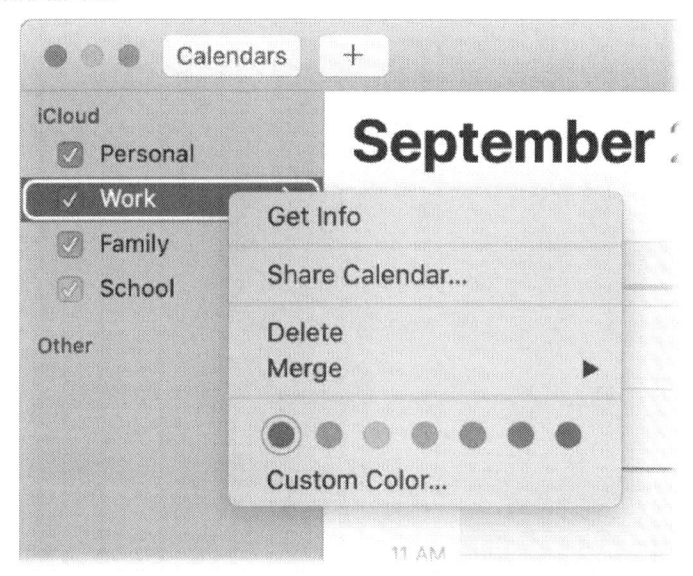

Share across your devices and with others. When you're signed in to iCloud, your calendars are kept up to date on all your Macs, iOS devices, iPadOS devices, and Apple Watch. You can also share calendars with other iCloud users.

Tip: If you add a location to an event, Calendar shows you a map, estimated travel time and time to leave, and even the weather forecast. Force click any event in Calendar to see more details.

FaceTime

Make video and audio calls from your Mac with FaceTime. **Ask Siri.** Say something like: "Make a FaceTime call to Sharon."

Video or audio only? Click the Video button to make a FaceTime video call. If it's not convenient to make a video call, click the Audio button to make an audio-only call.

When you receive a FaceTime invitation, you can choose to join with just video, just audio, or both.

Tip: While a video call is in progress, you can drag the small picture-in-picture window to any corner of the FaceTime window.

View your call log or missed calls.

Search or enter contact details.

List of recent calls

Leave a message. If your FaceTime video call is declined or not answered, click Message to send a text message.

Make a phone call. If you have an iPhone with iOS 8 or later, make phone calls from your Mac using FaceTime. Just make sure your Mac and iPhone are signed in with the same Apple ID account and that both have the feature turned on. (On your Mac, open FaceTime, choose FaceTime > Preferences, then select "Calls from iPhone.")

Note: A Wi-Fi connection is required in order to make or receive calls on your MacBook Air.

Find My

Use Find My to locate your friends, family, and Apple devices—all in the same app.

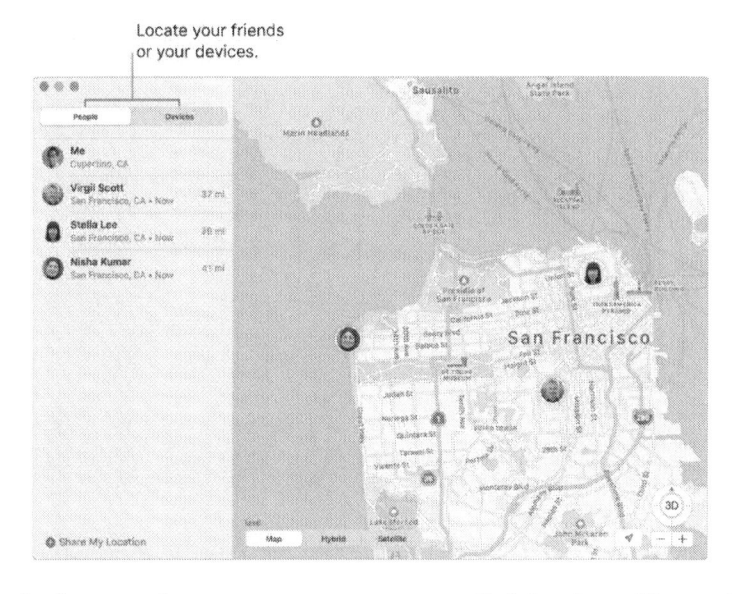

Note: Find My features are not available in all regions or languages.

Share locations with friends. In the People list, click Share My Location to tell friends and family where you are. You can share your location for an hour, a day, or indefinitely, and stop sharing whenever you like. You can also ask to follow a friend so you can see where they are on a map and get step-by-step directions to their location.

Set location alerts. Automatically send notifications to friends when you arrive at or leave a specific location. Set notifications when your friends leave and arrive, too. If your friends create notifications about your location, you can view them all in one place—click Me in the People list, then scroll to Notifications About You.

Secure a lost device. Use Find My to locate and protect a missing Mac, iPhone, iPad, iPod touch, Apple Watch, or AirPods. Click a device in the Devices list to locate it on the map. Click ⓘ to play a sound on the device to help you find it, mark the device as lost so others can't access your personal information, and even erase the device remotely.

Locate devices, even if they're offline. Find My uses Bluetooth signals from other nearby Apple devices to locate your device when it's not connected to a Wi-Fi or cellular network. These signals are anonymous and encrypted, and help find the location of your missing device without compromising privacy.

Find a family member's device. You can use Find My to help locate a family member's device, if you're in a Family Sharing group and your family member is sharing their location with you.

GarageBand

GarageBand is an app for creating, recording, and sharing your music. It has everything you need to learn to play an instrument, write music, or record a song—your own home recording studio.

Create a new project. You can start with a song template, select a tempo, key, and other options, then click Record and start playing. Build your song—for example, with different tracks and loops. Click Quick Help and hold the pointer over items to learn what they are and how they work.

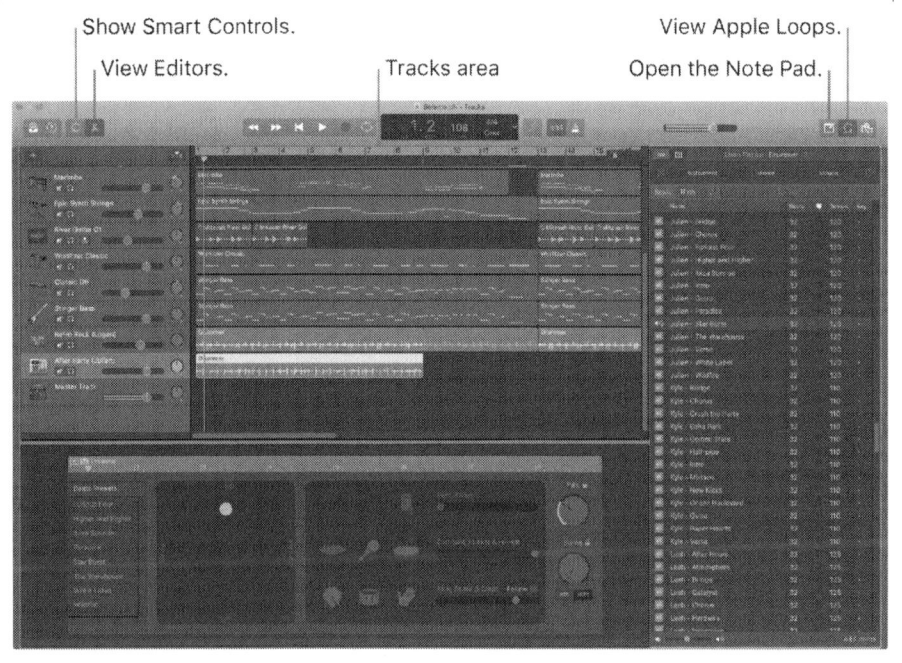

Bring in the beat. You can quickly add drums to your project using Drummer Loops. Click the Loop Browser ⌕, then drag a Drummer Loop into an empty part of the Tracks area. You can customize Drummer Loops to fit your song, using a simple set of controls.

Record your voice. Choose Track > New Track, then select the microphone under Audio. Click the triangle next to Details to set options for input, output, and monitoring, then click Create. Click the Record button ● to start recording, or the Play button ▶ to stop recording.

Home

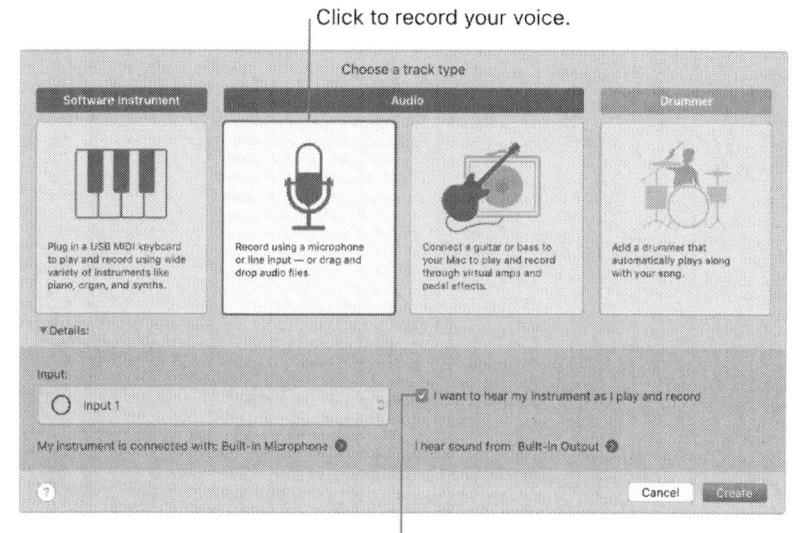

With the Home app, you can easily and securely control all of your HomeKit accessories from your Mac.

Accessory control. Accessories show up in the Home app as tiles with icons. Click an accessory tile to control it—turn lights on/off, lock/unlock the door, view live cameras, and more. You can also adjust the brightness of a light, or the target temperature of a thermostat.

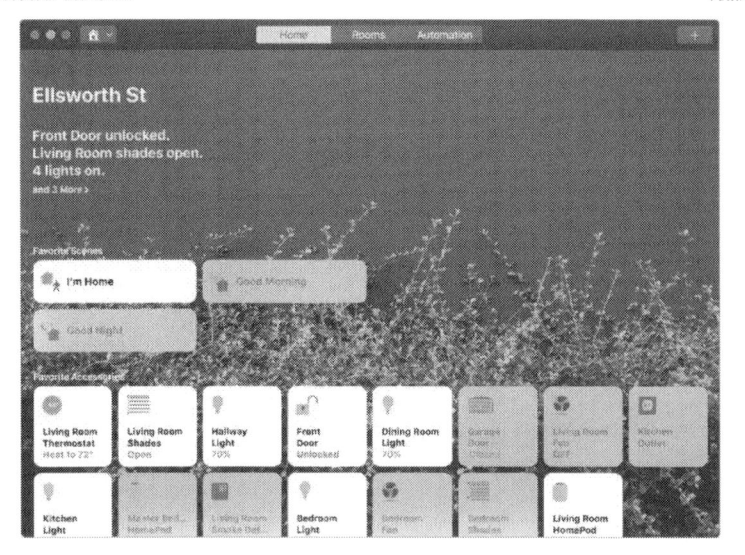

Shared Access. You can share your home with family members or guests, so they can control accessories using the Home app on their own Apple devices.

Create a scene. Create a scene that lets your accessories work together with a single command. For example, make a Good Night scene that turns off all the lights, closes the shades, and locks the door when you turn in for the night.

iMovie

iMovie lets you turn your home videos into beautiful movies and Hollywood-style trailers that you can share with a few quick clicks.

Import a video. Import video from your iPhone, iPad, or iPod touch, from a camera, or from media files already on your Mac. iMovie creates a new library and event for you.

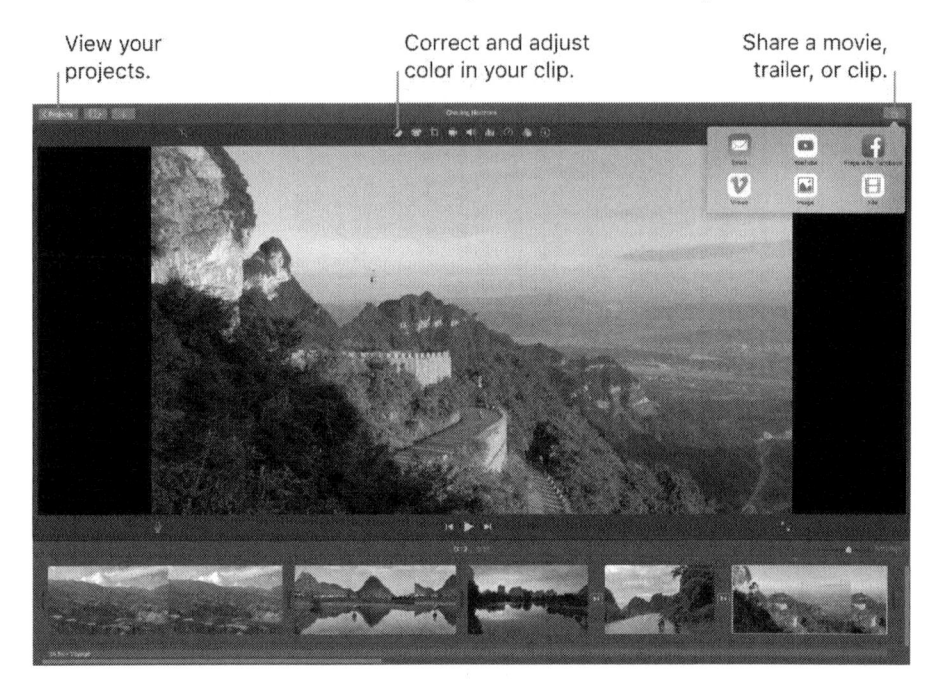

Record video with the built-in camera. Use the FaceTime HD camera on your Mac to record video and add it to your project. Select an event in the sidebar, click Import in the toolbar, select FaceTime HD Camera, then click the Record button to start and stop recording.

Create Hollywood-style trailers. Make clever trailers, complete with animated graphics and soaring soundtracks. Just add photos and video clips and customize the credits. To get started, click the New button ✛, click Trailer, choose a template from the Trailer window, then click Create. Add the cast and credits in the Outline tab, and add your own photos and videos in the Storyboard tab.

Click Play to preview the trailer.

Tip: Shooting video with a handheld device can produce shaky results, but you can stabilize the video so the playback is smoother. Select the shaky clip in the timeline, click the Stabilization button, then click Stabilize Shaky Video.

Keynote

Create professional, cutting-edge presentations with Keynote. Start with one of the more than 30 predesigned themes and make it your own by adding text, new objects, and changing the color scheme.

Organize visually. Use the slide navigator on the left to quickly add, rearrange, or delete slides. Click a slide to see it in the main window, drag a slide to change its order, or select a slide and press Delete to remove it.

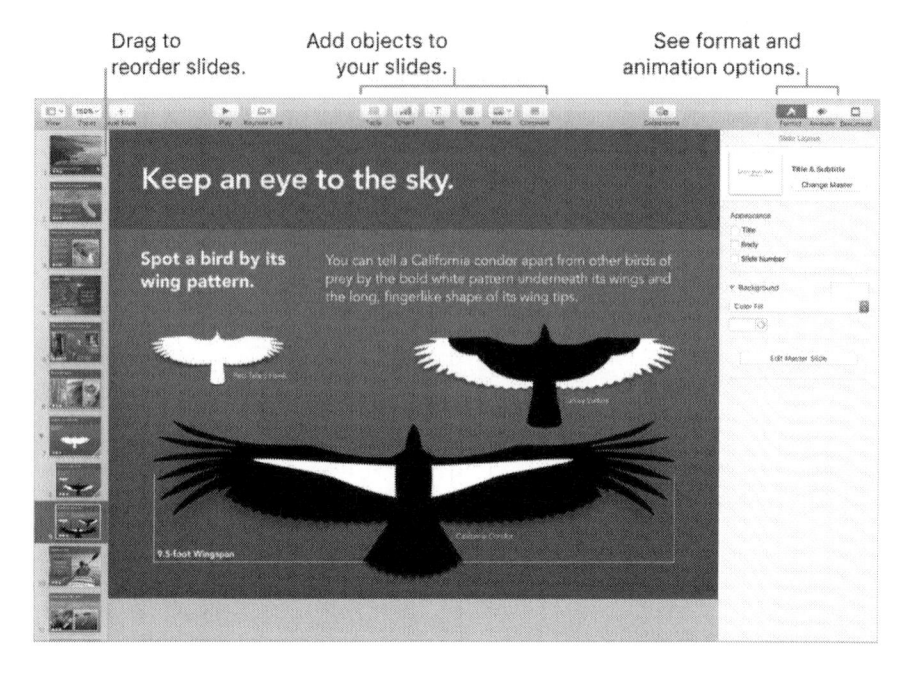

Practice makes perfect. To rehearse your presentation, choose Play > Rehearse Slideshow. You'll see each slide along with your notes—and a clock to keep you on track.

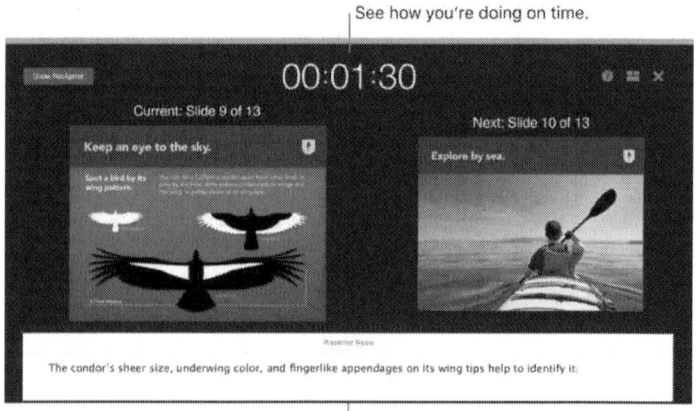

Share your presentation. If your manager wants to review your presentation or you want to share it with others on a conference call, choose Share > Send a Copy to send a copy by Mail, Messages, AirDrop, or even social media.

Draw them in. Get their attention by animating an object on a slide. Select the object, click Animate in the toolbar, click Action in the sidebar, then click Add an Effect.

Tip: You can include a video in your presentation. Click where you want it to be, then click the Media button in the toolbar. Click Movies, then find the movie you want and drag it to your slide.

Mail

Mail lets you manage all your email accounts from a single app. It works with most popular email services, such as iCloud, Gmail, Yahoo Mail, and AOL Mail.

One-stop email. Tired of signing in to multiple websites to check your email accounts? Set up Mail with all your accounts so you can see all your messages in one place. Choose Mail > Add Account.

Ask Siri. Say something like: "Any new mail from Laura today?" **Find the right message.** Type in the search field to see suggestions for messages that best match your query.

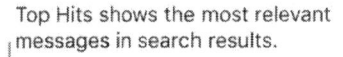

Focus on what's important. See only the messages you want to see in your inbox. You can block messages from specific senders by moving their messages directly to the Trash, mute overly active email threads, and unsubscribe from mailing lists directly in Mail.

Add events and contacts right from Mail. When you receive a message that includes a new email address or event, just click Add to add it to Contacts or Calendar. Force click an address to see a preview of the location, which you can open in Maps.

Personalize any message. Add emoji or photos with just a click. Select photos from your photo library or take them on iPhone or iPad. You can also add a sketch you've drawn on your iPhone or iPad.

Add photos.

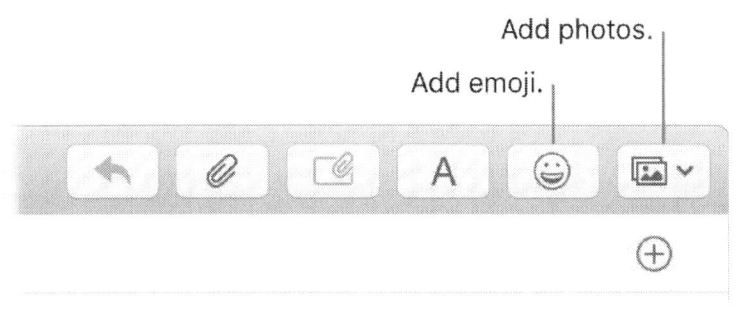

Add emoji.

View in full screen. When you're using Mail in full screen, windows for new messages automatically open in Split View on the right, so it's easy to reference another message in your inbox as you write.

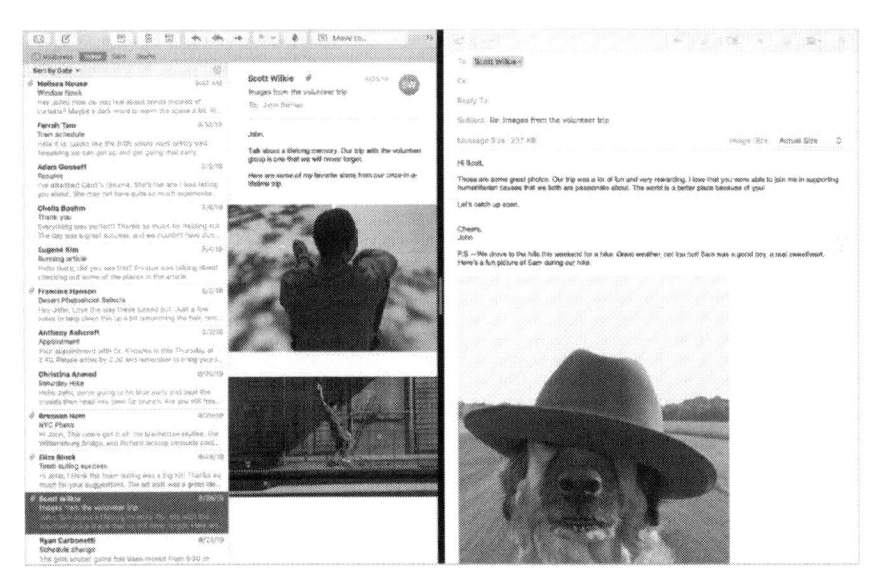

Never miss an email. Check the Mail icon in the Dock to see the number of unread messages. When you get a new email, a notification also appears at the top-right of the screen so you can quickly preview incoming messages. (Don't want notifications? To turn them off, open System Preferences, then click Notifications.)

Maps

Get directions and view locations using a map or a satellite image. Or use Flyover to view select cities in 3D. Force click a location to drop a pin there.

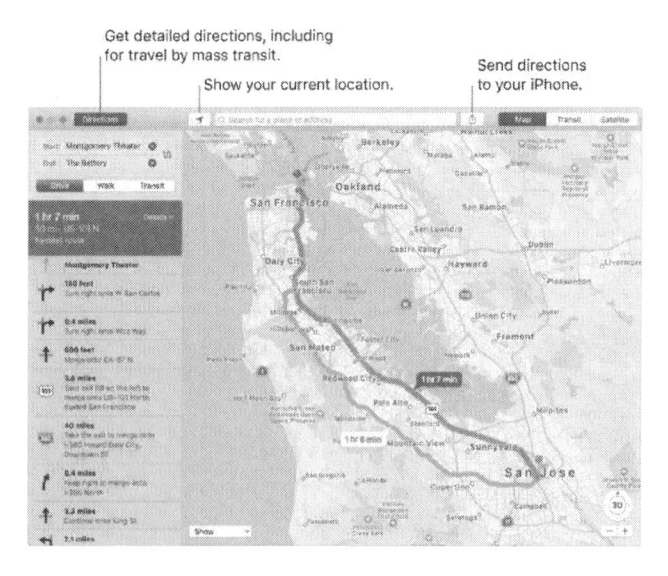

Let iPhone show you the way. Click Directions to find the best route to your destination, then click the Share button to send the directions to your iPhone for turn-by-turn voice navigation.

Get there on public transit. Maps provides public transit information for select cities. Click Transit, then click a destination to get suggested travel routes and estimated travel time.

More than just maps. For local points of interest such as hotels and restaurants, Maps shows you addresses, phone numbers, photos, and even reviews.

Ask Siri. Say something like: "Find coffee near me."

Tip: To see what traffic is like, click the Show pop-up menu in the bottom left of the map, then choose Show Traffic.

Maps

Get directions and view locations using a map or a satellite image. Or use Flyover to view select cities in 3D. Force click a location to drop a pin there.

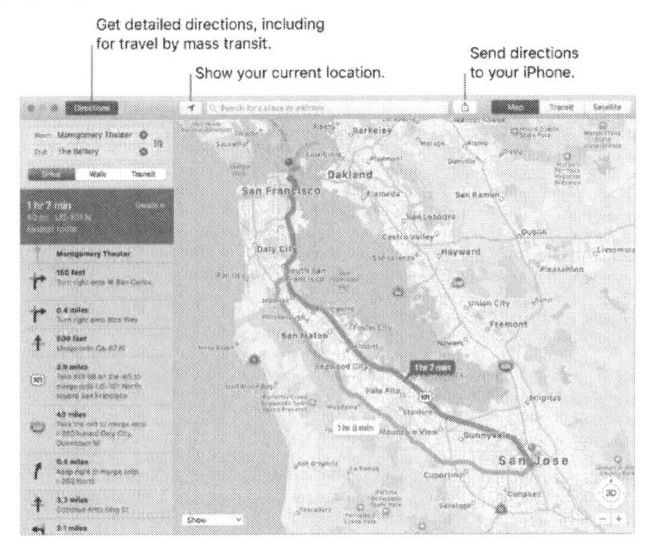

Let iPhone show you the way. Click Directions to find the best route to your destination, then click the Share button to send the directions to your iPhone for turn-by-turn voice navigation.

Get there on public transit. Maps provides public transit information for select cities. Click Transit, then click a destination to get suggested travel routes and estimated travel time.

More than just maps. For local points of interest such as hotels and restaurants, Maps shows you addresses, phone numbers, photos, and even reviews.

Ask Siri. Say something like: "Find coffee near me."

Tip: To see what traffic is like, click the Show pop-up menu in the bottom left of the map, then choose Show Traffic.

Messages

With Messages, it's easy to stay in touch. Connect with one or more people through text, audio, or video. And if you want to share files, you can do that too.

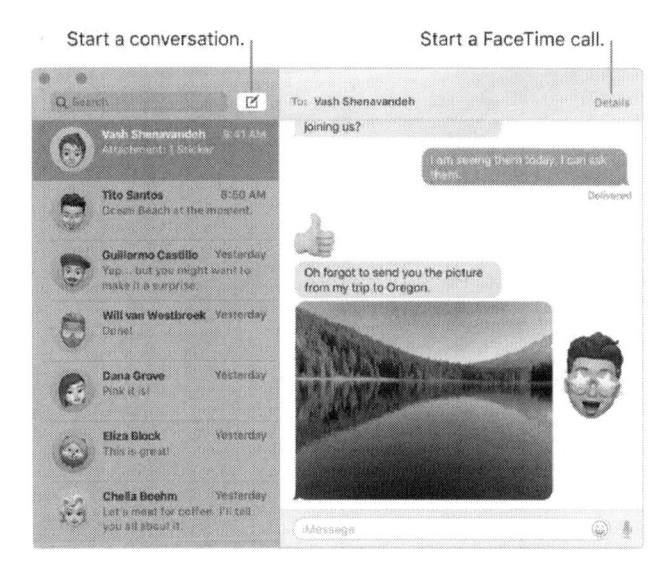

Sign in and send. Sign in with your Apple ID to exchange unlimited messages—including text, photos, Live Photos, video, and more—with anyone with a Mac, iPhone, iPad, iPod touch, or Apple Watch.

Tip: You can also send and receive SMS and MMS messages on your Mac, if your iPhone (with iOS 8.1 or later) is signed in to

Messages with the same Apple ID. On your iPhone, go to Settings > Messages, tap Text Message Forwarding, then tap the name of your Mac to turn on Text Message Forwarding. On your Mac, you'll see an activation code. Enter this on your iPhone, then tap Allow.

Ask Siri. Say something like: "Message Mom that I'll be late."

Make messages fun. Liven up discussions by responding to messages with large emoji or Tapbacks. To add a Tapback, click and hold a message, then choose a Tapback. And look out for stickers, Digital Touch, invisible ink, and handwritten messages that your friends send you from their iOS device, iPadOS device, or Apple Watch.

When a text isn't enough. If your friend also has FaceTime, you can start a FaceTime video or audio chat right from a conversation in Messages. Just click Details in the message window, then click the Video button ▇◢ or Audio button ☎.

Share your screen. You can share your screen with a friend—and vice versa—and even open folders, create documents, and copy files by dragging them to the desktop on the shared screen. Click Details, then click the Screen Share button .

Music

The Apple Music app makes it easy to organize and enjoy your iTunes Store purchases, songs, and albums in your personal library, and in the Apple Music catalog (which lets you listen to millions of songs on demand). Click to view what's next, previously played tracks, and lyrics for what's playing. Shop for the music you want in the iTunes Store.

It's in your library. You can easily view and play your iTunes Store purchases, items you added from the Apple Music catalog, and music in your personal library. Filter your content by Recently Added, Artists, Albums, or Songs.

Browse the best of Apple Music. Click Browse to see new music and exclusive releases from Apple Music, a music streaming service available for a monthly fee. Stream and download more than 50 million songs ad-free, and choose from a large selection of playlists to find the perfect mix for any moment.

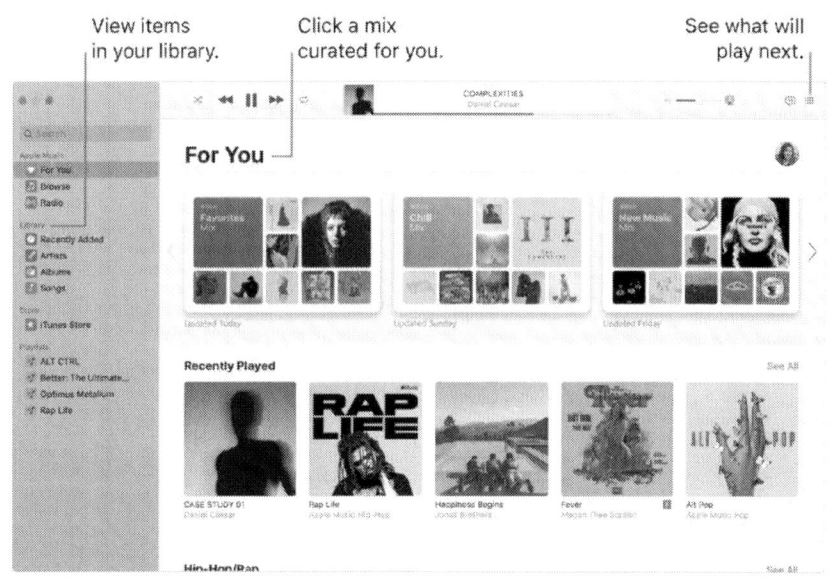

Sing along. Click 💬 to display a panel with lyrics for the current song (if available).

Tune in. Click Radio to tune in to Beats 1 live or listen to any episode from the Beats 1 family of shows. Explore the variety of stations created for almost every genre of music.

Ask Siri. Say something like: "Play Beats 1."

Sync with ease. Sync your music content directly in the Apple Music app. When you connect a device, you see it in the sidebar of the Finder. Just drag the content you want onto your device. You can also back up and restore your device in the Finder.

Buy it on the iTunes Store. If you want to own your music, click iTunes Store in the sidebar. (If you don't see the store in the sidebar, choose Music > Preferences, click General, then click Show iTunes Store.)

Tip: When screen real estate is at a premium, switch to MiniPlayer to open a small floating window that you can drag where you want, so you can listen and control your music while doing other things on your Mac. To open MiniPlayer, choose Window > Switch to MiniPlayer, click 📇, or press Shift-Command-M.

News

Apple News is your one-stop destination for trusted news and information, curated by editors and personalized for you. You can save articles for future reading—even offline or on other devices. Apple News+ lets you read hundreds of magazines, popular newspapers, and premium digital publishers for a single monthly price.

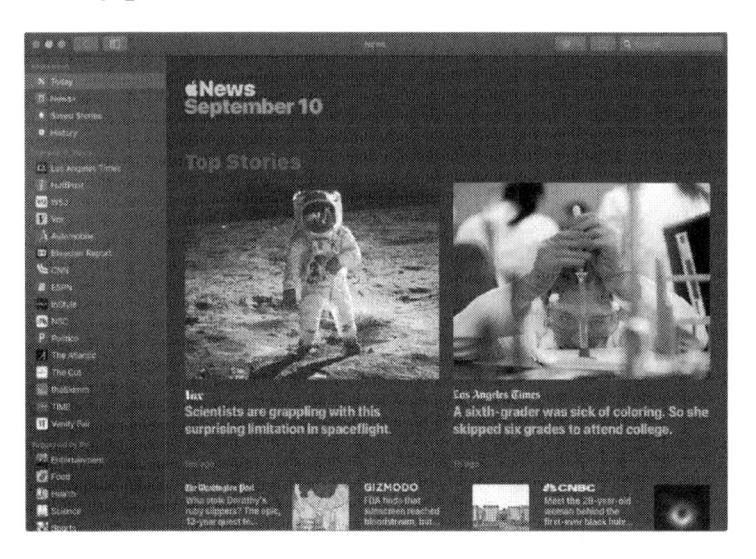

Note: Apple News and Apple News+ are not available in all countries or regions.

Customize your feed. Follow your favorite channels and topics to see them in the Today feed and sidebar. Enter a news outlet or topic in the search field, then click ♡ to follow it.

Navigate easily with the sidebar. Use the sidebar to quickly choose a channel or topic. To adjust the order of the sidebar contents, click Edit, then use the handle to drag and drop the channels and topics into the order you prefer.

Tip: If you're reading an article and want to save it for later, choose File > Save Story. To view the article later, click Saved Stories at the bottom of the sidebar. You can access articles from any of your devices when you sign in with the same Apple ID.

Notes

Notes are more than just text. Jot down quick thoughts, or add checklists, images, web links, and more. Shared folders let you share an entire folder of notes with a group, and everyone can participate. Powerful new search optimizations help you find the right notes more quickly.

Ask Siri. Say something like: "Create a new note."

View your notes a new way. Gallery view allows you to see your notes as visual thumbnails, making it easier than ever to quickly navigate to the note you're looking for.

Share folders. You can now share entire folders—including all the notes and subfolders inside. Share an entire folder with your family or team, giving everyone access so they can create or edit notes, add attachments, and even create subfolders. Click the Add People button and select a method for sending the link.

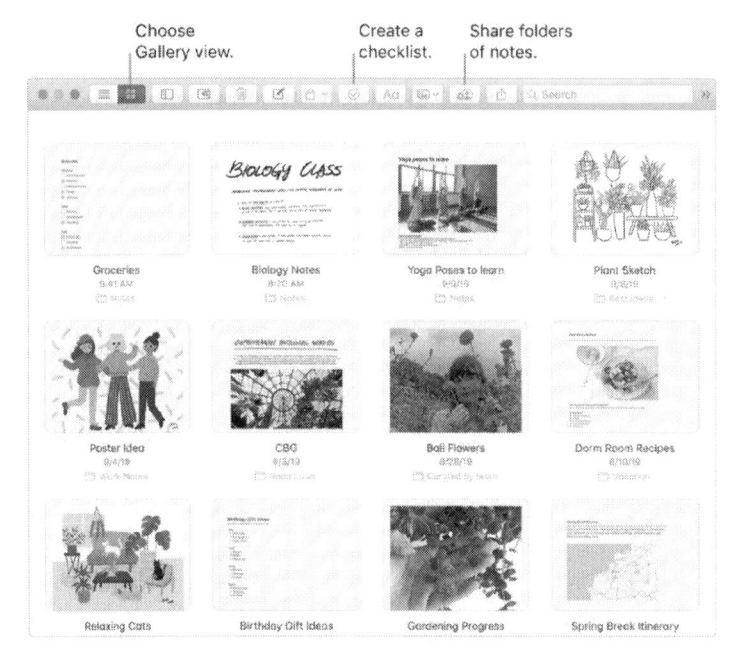

Tip: When you're signed in with your Apple ID and iCloud is turned on for Notes, your notes are kept up to date on all your devices—so you can create a to-do list on your Mac, then check off items on your iPhone while you're on the go.

Check off your list. Click the Checklist button ⊘ to add an interactive checklist to a note, which automatically sends checked items to the bottom of the list. Choose Format > More > Uncheck All to uncheck all the items in your list and start over—perfect for reusing your weekly shopping lists.

Add photos, videos, and more. Drag a photo, video, PDF, or other document from the desktop. Choose Window > Photo Browser to add items from your Photos library to a note.

Add a table. Click the Table button ⊞ to add a table to your note. You can even copy a table from a website or another app and paste it into your note.

Lock a note. You can lock a note with a password to make sure that only those who know the password can see the note. To lock a note, choose Notes > Preferences and click Set Password. Then select the note you want to lock, and choose File > Lock This Note.

Numbers

Use Numbers to create attractive and powerful spreadsheets on your Mac. More than 30 Apple-designed templates give you a head start creating budgets, invoices, team rosters, and more. Numbers can also open and export Microsoft Excel spreadsheets.

Start with a template—then add what you want. Select the sample text in the template, then type new text. To add images, drag a graphic file from your Mac to the placeholder image.

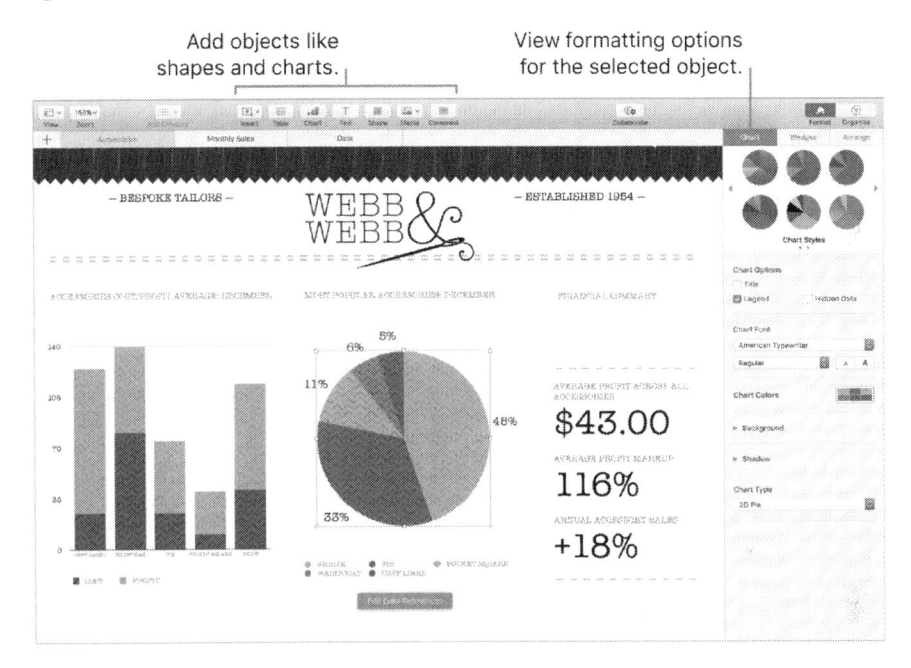

Get organized with sheets. Use multiple sheets or tabs to show different views of your information. For example, use one sheet for your budget, another for a table, and a third for notes. Click + to add a new sheet. Drag a tab left or right to reorder sheets.

Formulas are a snap. Get built-in help for more than 250 powerful functions—just type the equal sign (=) in a cell, and you see a list of all the functions and their descriptions in the sidebar. Start typing a formula to get instant suggestions.

Tip: To get instant calculations on a series of values, select the range of cells containing the values. At the bottom of the window you'll see the sum, average, minimum, maximum, and count of the selected values. Click the Settings button ⚙ to see even more options.

Pages

Use the Pages app to create stunning, media-rich documents on your Mac. Open and edit Microsoft Word files, and easily share a link to your work in Mail or Messages, right from the toolbar.

Look good! Pages includes a variety of beautiful templates for flyers, newsletters, reports, and résumés, among others, making it easy to start your project.

All your formatting tools, in one place. Click the Format button 🔨 in the toolbar to open the Format inspector. Select something in your document, and the formatting options for it appear.

Flow text around graphics. When you add an image to a text document, the text flows automatically around the image. You can fine-tune how the text wraps in the Format sidebar.

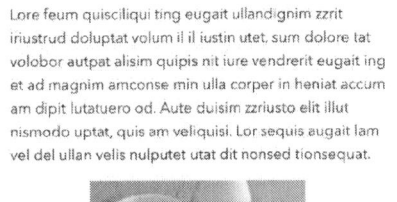

Move a graphic into a text block...  ...and the text wraps around the graphic automatically.

Start on your Mac, finish on iPad. You can keep documents up to date across all your devices when you sign in with the same Apple ID. So you can start composing on one device, and pick up where you left off on another.

Tip: Turn on change tracking to see the changes you and others make to a document. Each person's edits and comments are color-coded, so you can see who made the change. Choose Edit > Turn on Tracking to show the change tracking toolbar.

Photos

Use Photos and iCloud Photos to organize, edit, and share your photos and videos, and keep your entire photo library up to date on all your devices. With Photos, it's easy to organize albums, find just the photo that you're looking for, and make beautiful slideshows and photo gifts.

All-new Photos tab. View your new photos and memories by day, month, or year. It's easier than ever to relive a specific moment by finding photos from that day—or click All Photos to quickly view your entire collection.

Relive meaningful moments. New Live Photos and videos that begin playing as you scroll bring your memories to life. Animations and transitions keep your place in the timeline switching between views, so you can switch between any view—like Days and All Photos—without losing your place.

People and Places. Photos understands your photos—who's in them and what's happening—and highlights important moments like birthdays, anniversaries, and trips. Make someone a favorite by clicking the Favorite button ♡ that appears on their photo, and they'll always appear at the top of the album. Use the Places album to view all your photos with location data on an interactive map. Zoom in on the map to reveal more photos from a specific location.

Tip: You can add location info to any photo. While viewing the photo, click the Information button ⓘ, click Assign a Location, then start typing. Choose your location from the list, or type it and press Return.

Find the perfect shot. Search your photos based on what's in them, the date they were taken, people you've named in them, and their location—if provided. Photos identifies objects, scenes, and people, so you don't have to use keywords to tag each photo.

Ask Siri. Say something like: "Show me photos of Sally."

Best shots. Photos intelligently showcases the best shots in your library, removing duplicates and clutter.

Memory Movies. Now you can view Memory Movies on your Mac, and edit the duration, mood, and title. Edits sync to your other devices using iCloud Photos. Memory titles add additional fonts and avoid overlapping faces.

Get lively. With Live Photos, use the new Loop effect to continuously loop the action, or use Bounce to play the animation forward and backward. You can also use Long Exposure to blur motion in your Live Photos.

Podcasts

Use Apple Podcast to browse, subscribe, and listen to favorite podcasts on your Mac.

Get started with Listen Now. Any podcasts you're in the middle of will be saved in Listen Now, even if you started listening from another device. You'll also see new episodes for the podcasts you're subscribed to, as well as personalized recommendations for podcasts you might be interested in.

Ask Siri. Say something like: "Continue playing the last podcast."

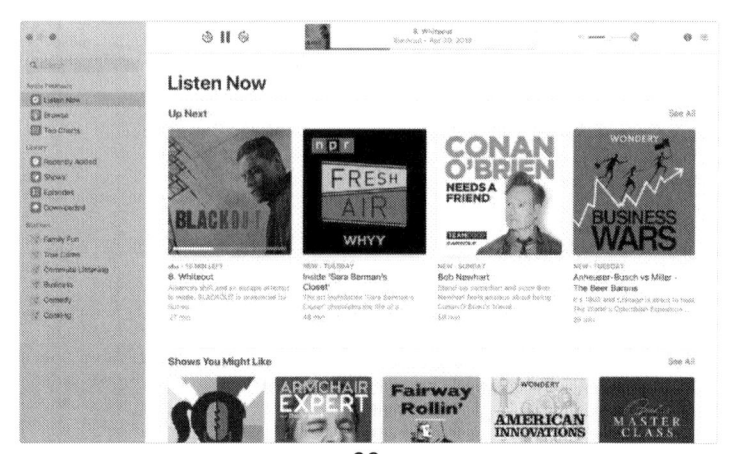

Save episodes to your library. To save a single episode to your library, click ✛. To keep up with new episodes for an entire podcast, click Subscribe. To download a podcast for offline listening, click ☁.

Discover new podcasts. Find a curated feed of new podcasts in Browse, or see which shows are trending in Top Charts. If you see a show you like, subscribe to the podcast or add an episode to your library for later.

Search by host or guest. When you search for a specific topic or person, you can see results for shows they host, shows that they're a guest on, and even shows where they're mentioned or discussed.

Tip: To play music or radio from a speaker using AirPlay, click the AirPlay icon ⏶ in the menu bar and select an available speaker.

Reminders

Reminders makes it easier than ever to keep track of all of your to-dos. Create and organize reminders for grocery lists, projects at work, or anything else you want to track. You can also choose when and where to receive reminders.

Keep track with smart lists. Smart lists automatically sort your upcoming reminders into four categories. Select Today to see all your reminders scheduled for today, as well as any overdue reminders. Select Scheduled to see your reminders with dates and times in one chronological view. Select Flagged to see reminders you've marked as important. Select All to see all your reminders in one place.

Work quickly with edit buttons. When you type, edit buttons appear below the reminder. Add dates, times, and locations so you can be reminded when and where you want. Click the flag icon ⚑ to mark a reminder as important.

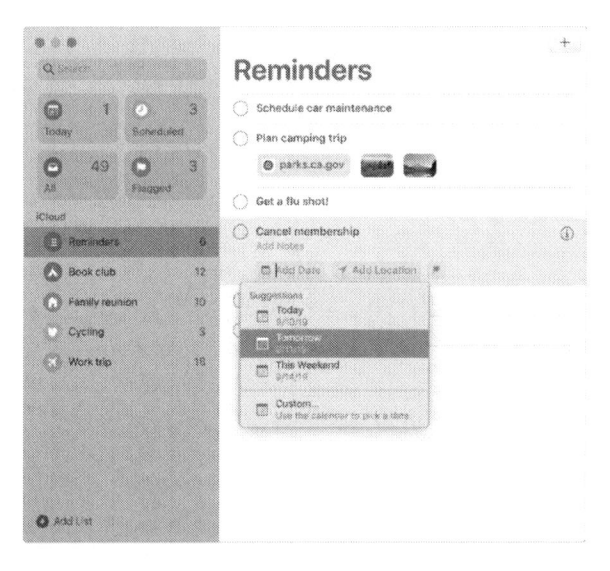

Add attachments. Make your reminders more useful by attaching photos, document scans, or links. To add an attachment, click the Edit Details button ⓘ, then choose Add image or Add URL. Or drag attachments from other apps, such as an event from Calendar.

Organize with subtasks and groups. To turn a reminder into a subtask, press Command-], or drag it on top of another reminder. The parent reminder becomes bold, and the subtask is indented underneath it. You can collapse or expand your subtasks to keep your view uncluttered.

To group reminders together, choose File > New Group. Name the group whatever you'd like. Add more lists by dragging them into the group, or remove them by dragging them out.

Customize list appearance. Double-click the icon of the list you want to customize. Click the icon in the info menu, then pick your preferred colors and symbols.

Use Siri to create reminders. Just type your reminder, and Siri understands more detailed sentences and provides relevant suggestions for when to remind you. Or you can ask Siri to schedule a reminder for you. For example, say "Remind me to call Mom at eight."

Be reminded when you text. Click the Edit Details button ⓘ , select When Messaging a Person, and enter someone's name. The next time you chat with them in Messages, you'll be reminded that now might be a good time to talk.

Safari

Safari is the fastest and most efficient way to surf the web on your Mac. An updated start page includes Favorites, frequently and recently visited websites, Siri Suggestions for relevant websites in your browsing history, bookmarks, Reading List, iCloud tabs, and links sent to you in Messages.

Start searching. Click the Smart Search field at the top of the window to see websites you've added as favorites. Or start typing a word or website address—Safari shows you matching websites, as well as Safari Suggestions.

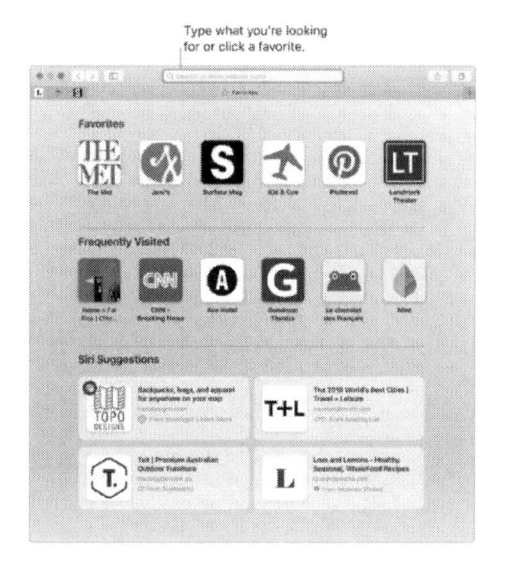

View multiple websites in one window. Click ＋ at the far right of the tab bar or press Command-T to open a new tab, then enter an address. To keep a website handy, drag its tab left to pin it, and it stays in the tab bar.

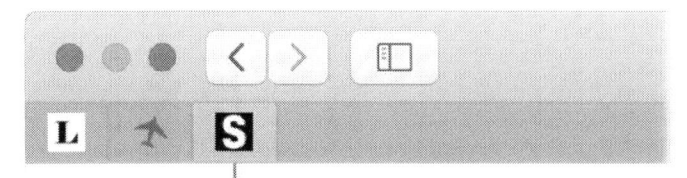

Drag a tab to the left
to pin it in the tab bar.

See what's open on each of your devices. You can see open webpages on all your devices that are signed in to the same Apple ID. Just click the Show All Tabs button at the top of the window and scroll down if necessary.

Browse the web safely and privately. Safari warns you when you visit a website that's not secure, or that may be trying to trick you into sharing your personal data. Safari also protects you automatically from cross-site tracking, by identifying and removing the data that trackers leave behind. Safari asks your permission before allowing a social network to see what you're doing on third-party sites. For example, if you click a Facebook button to share an article to Facebook, Safari asks if you want to let Facebook see your activity on the site. And Safari defends you against web tracking by making your Mac harder to identify uniquely.

When you sign up for a new account on the web, Safari automatically creates and autofills a new strong password for you. If you choose Use Strong Password, the password is saved to your iCloud Keychain and will autofill on all the devices you log in to with the same Apple ID. You can ask Siri to show you your saved passwords, which you can see after entering the authentication password for your Mac, or go to Safari > Preferences and then click Passwords. Reused passwords are flagged in the passwords list, so you can easily replace them with strong passwords.

Ask Siri. Say something like: "Show me my password."

Note: Siri may not be available in all languages or in all areas, and features may vary by area.

Set up preferences for your favorite sites. If you often adjust settings for certain websites, you can use Safari preferences to save those settings. You can turn on your content blocker, enable Reader mode, allow notifications, set a specific page zoom, and more—just for the websites you choose. When you're visiting a website, choose Safari > Settings for This Website, or secondary click (that is, right-click) on the URL in the Smart Search field.

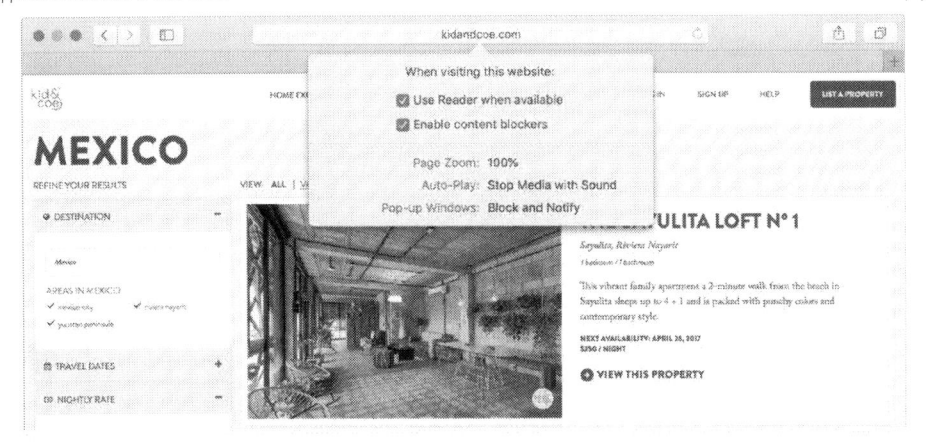

Tip: In a webpage, force click a word to see its definition, or a Wikipedia article if one is available. Try force clicking text in other apps, like Messages or Mail, to get more info.

Open Picture in Picture. When you're playing a video, click and hold the Audio button 🔊 on the tab and choose Enter Picture in Picture from the submenu. Your video appears in a floating window that you can drag and resize, so you can watch while doing other things on your Mac. You can also set autoplay options in this submenu. To mute the sound from a video, click 🔊).

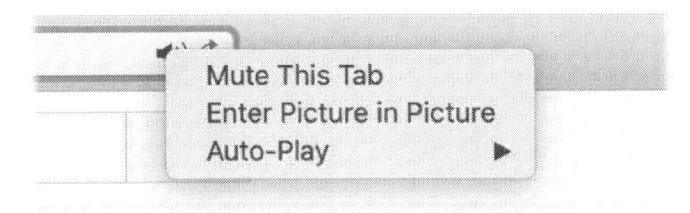

Stocks

The Stocks app is the best way to track the market on your Mac. View prices in the custom watchlist, click a stock to see more details and an interactive chart, and read about what's driving the market, with stories from Apple News.

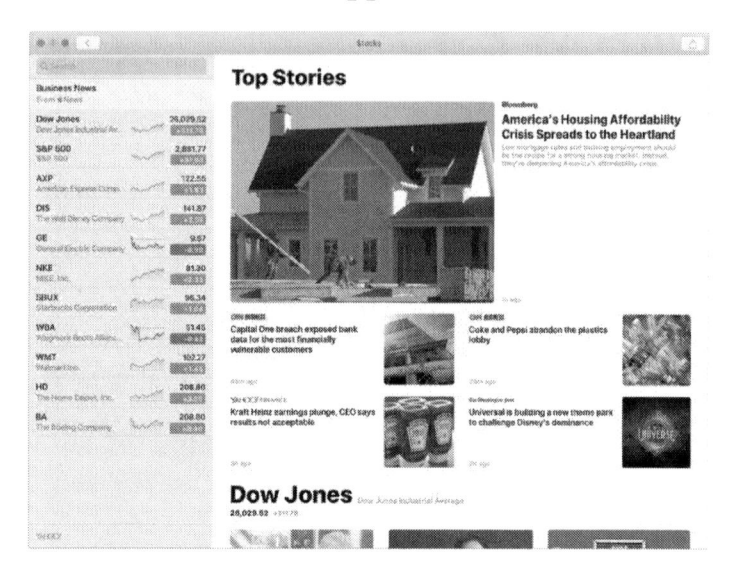

Note: Apple News stories and Top Stories are available in the U.S., Canada, the UK, and Australia. News stories in other countries and regions are provided by Yahoo.

Customize your watchlist. Click the edit button at the bottom of the list to customize stocks, indexes, currencies, and more. While viewing your watchlist, click the green or red button below each price to cycle between price change, percentage change, and market capitalization. The watchlist also includes color-coded sparklines that track performance throughout the day.

Read articles related to the companies you follow. Click a stock in your watchlist to see an interactive chart and additional details, and read the latest news about that company.

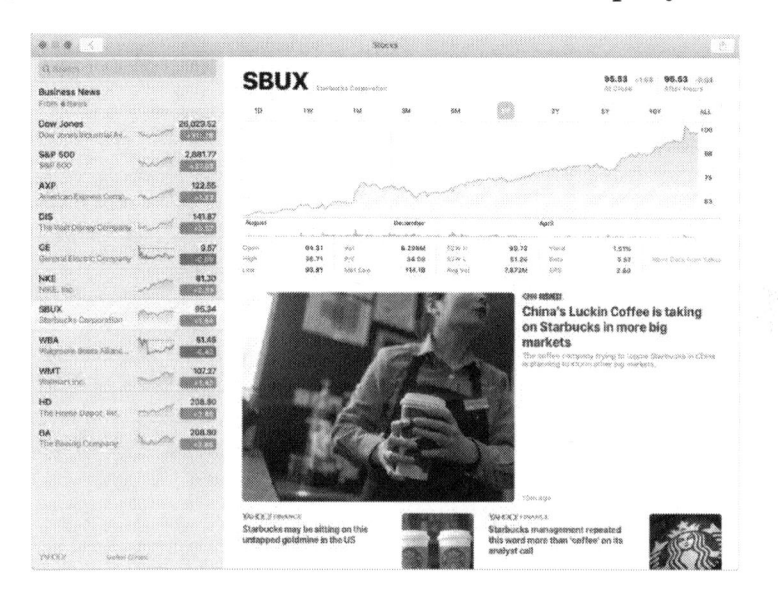

Get a deeper view. Want to see what the market was doing last week, last month, or last year? Click the buttons above the chart to switch timeframes and see prices in the view you like best.

Your watchlist on all your devices. Keep your watchlist consistent across all your devices when you sign in with the same Apple ID.

Tip: Click the Top Stories section in the watchlist to see a collection of timely business articles, curated by Apple News editors.

TV

Watch all your movies and TV shows in the Apple TV app. Buy or rent movies and TV shows, subscribe to channels, and pick up where you left off watching from any of your devices.

Get started with Watch Now. In Watch Now, browse a curated feed of recommendations, based on channels you're subscribed to and movies or TV shows you've watched.

Keep watching in Up Next. In Up Next, you'll find movies or TV shows you're watching, as well as movies and TV shows you've added to your queue. To add a new movie or TV show to Up Next, click the Add to Up Next button.

Discover more in Movies, TV Shows, and Kids. If you're looking for something specific, click the Movies, TV Shows, or Kids tab in the menu bar, then browse by genre.

Buy, rent, or subscribe. When you find a movie or TV show you want to watch, you can choose to buy or rent it. Channels you've subscribed to are available on all devices, and can be used by up to six family members through Family Sharing.

Choose something from your own library. Click Library to see all the movies and TV shows you've purchased or downloaded, organized by genre. To start watching, just click the movie or TV show.

Voice Memos

Voice Memos makes it easier than ever to capture personal reminders, class lectures, and even interviews or song ideas. With iCloud, you can access the voice memos you record with your iPhone, right on your MacBook Air.

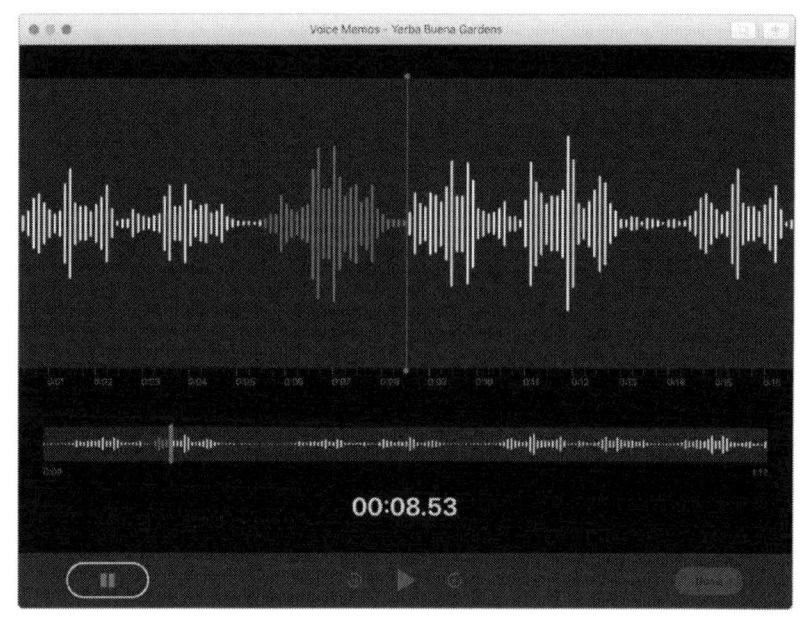

Record from your MacBook Air. To record, click the red button. To stop recording, click Done. Name your recordings to keep them organized by typing in the name field. Play back your recording by clicking the play button.

Your voice memos across all your devices. Your voice memos are available on all your devices when you sign in with the same Apple ID. You can access recordings you made with your iPhone or iPad right from your Mac.

Keyboard shortcuts on your Mac

You can press key combinations to do things on your MacBook Air that you'd normally do with a trackpad, mouse, or other device. Here's a list of commonly used keyboard shortcuts.

Shortcut   Description

Shortcut	Description
Command-X	Cut the selected item and copy it to the Clipboard.
Command-C	Copy the selected item to the Clipboard.
Command-V	Paste the contents of the Clipboard into the current document or app.
Command-Z	Undo the previous command. Press Command-Shift-Z to redo.
Command-A	Select all items.
Command-F	Open a Find window, or find items in a document.
Command-G	Find the next occurrence of the item you're searching for. Press Command-Shift-G to find the previous occurrence.
Command-H	Hide the windows of the front app. Press Command-Option-H to view the front app but hide all other apps.
Command-M	Minimize the front window to the Dock. Press Command-Option-M to minimize all windows of the front app.
Command-N	Open a new document or window.

Shortcut	Description
Command-O	Open the selected item, or open a dialog to select a file to open.
Command-P	Print the current document.
Command-S	Save the current document.
Command-W	Close the front window. Press Command-Option-W to close all windows of the app.
Command-Q	Quit the current app.
Command-Option-Esc	Choose an app to Force Quit.
Command-Tab	Switch to the next most recently used app among your open apps.
Command-Shift-5	Open the Screenshot utility. You can also take screenshots using the following shortcuts: • Press Command-Shift-3 to take a screenshot of the entire screen. • Press Command-Shift-4 to take a screenshot of a selected area of the screen.

Save space on your MacBook Air

With Optimize Storage, you can automatically free up space on your MacBook Air by making files available on demand. Your oldest files will be stored in iCloud and on your email IMAP or Exchange server, so you can download them at any time. There are also tools to identify and delete big files.

Optimize storage. To see storage recommendations, go to Apple menu > About This Mac, click Storage, then click Manage. You'll see different recommendations based on how you configured your Mac. If your Mac is low on storage, you'll see an alert with a link to the Storage pane.

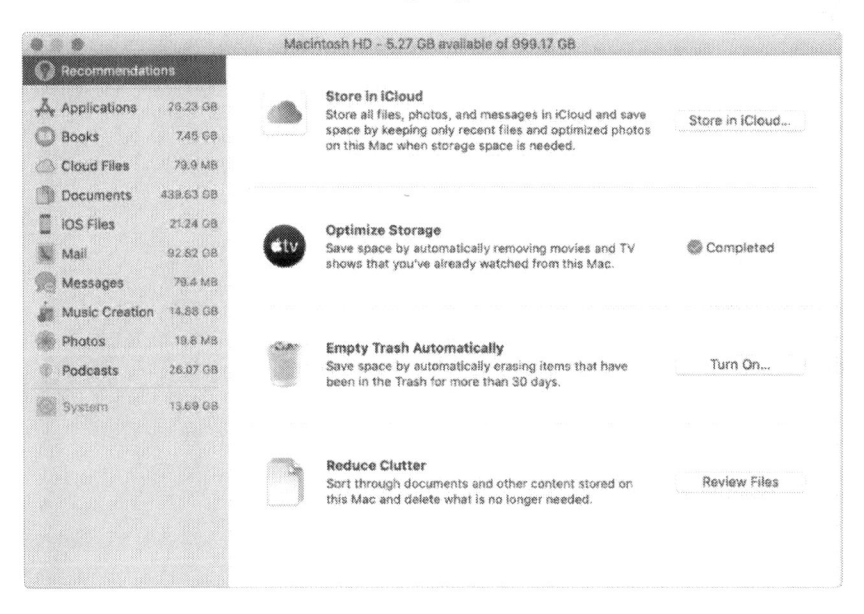

Set options to:

- *Store in iCloud:* Store all files, photos, and messages in iCloud and save space on your Mac.
    - *Desktop and Documents:* Store all the files from your Desktop and Documents folders in iCloud Drive. When storage space is needed,

iCloud Drive keeps recently opened files on your Mac and makes your oldest files available on demand.

- *Photos:* Store photos and videos in iCloud Photos. When storage spaces is needed, iCloud Photos uses optimized versions of photos and video on your Mac and makes the originals available on demand.
- *Messages:* Store all messages and attachments in iCloud. When storage space is needed, iCloud keeps recent attachments on your Mac and makes your oldest files available on demand.

Even though your files are stored in the cloud, you can access them right where you left them on your MacBook Air.

- *Optimize Storage:* Save space on your Mac by optimizing the storage of movies and TV shows in the Apple TV app. You can choose to automatically remove movies or TV shows from your MacBook Air after you watch them. You can download them again at any time.
- *Empty Trash Automatically:* Automatically erase items that have been in the Trash for more than 30 days.
- *Reduce Clutter:* Easily identify large files, and delete the files you no longer need. To browse large files, click through the categories in the sidebar—

Documents, Applications, Mail, Messages, Books, iCloud Drive, and more.

To help you save space as you work, macOS also:

- Prevents you from downloading the same file twice from Safari

- Alerts you to remove installer software when you finish installing a new app

- Clears logs and caches that are safe to remove when you're low on storage

Take a screenshot on your Mac

- Explore the Screenshot menu to find all the controls you need to take screenshots and screen recordings. You can also capture your voice during a screen recording. The optimized workflow lets you take photos and videos of your screen, and then easily share, edit, or save them.

- **Access the screenshot controls.** Press Command-Shift-5. You can capture the entire screen, a selected window, or a portion of a window. You can also record the entire screen or a selected portion of the screen.

- Use the icons at the bottom of the screen to capture a selection, record your screen, and more. Click Options to modify your save location, set a timer before capturing, set microphone and audio options, or show the pointer. Click Capture to take the screenshot.

- After you take a screenshot or video, a thumbnail appears in the corner of the screen. Drag the thumbnail into a document or folder, swipe to the right to quickly save it, or click to edit or share it.
- *Note:* You can also open the Screenshot utility from the Other folder in Launchpad, or in the Apps/Utilities folder in the Finder.
- **Mark up your screenshot.** Click the thumbnail of your screenshot to use Markup tools and make annotations. You can also click Share to send your marked up screen to colleagues or friends—right from the screenshot itself.

Chapter 5
Maximizing the Apps
Apps included on your Mac

Your Mac comes with a wide range of apps already installed so you can have fun, work, connect with friends, get organized, buy things, and more. To open apps, click their icons in the Dock or click the Launchpad icon in the Dock, then use Launchpad to open apps.

Tip: Every app that comes with your Mac includes help so you can become a pro using it. Just choose Help in the menu bar while using the app.

You can change the look of the menu bar, desktop picture, Dock, and built-in apps appearance in System Preferences.

During downtime, or if you reach the time limit set for apps in Screen Time preferences, app icons are dimmed and an hourglass icon is shown.

Use Launchpad to view and open apps on Mac

Launchpad on your Mac is a central location where you can see and open apps that are on your Mac.

Open and close Launchpad

- *Open Launchpad:* Click its icon in the Dock(or use the Control Strip).

- *Close Launchpad without opening an app:* Click anywhere (except on an app) or press Esc.

Find and open apps in Launchpad

- *Find an app:* Type its name in the search field at the top of Launchpad. Or look on another page in Launchpad—swipe left or right on the trackpad or press Command-Left Arrow or Command-Right Arrow.

- *Open an app:* Click it.

During downtime, or if you reach the time limit set for apps in Screen Time preferences, app icons are dimmed and an hourglass icon ⌛ is shown.

Organize apps in Launchpad

- *Move an app on a page:* Drag an app to a new location on the same page.

- *Move an app to another page:* Drag the app to the edge of the screen, then release it when the page you want appears.

- *Create an app folder:* Drag an app over another app. To add another app, drag it over the folder. To remove an app, drag it out of the folder.

    Tip: Don't like the name of a folder? Click the folder to open it, click its name, and then type a new name.

Add apps to Launchpad

Apps that you download from the App Store automatically appear in Launchpad.

Add an app that you didn't download from the App Store: Drag the app to the Applications folder in the Finderon your Mac. The app is then shown in Launchpad.

Remove apps from Launchpad

1. In Launchpad, click and hold an app until all the apps begin to jiggle.

2. Click the app's Delete button ⊗.

    If you don't see a Delete button, the app can't be removed from Launchpad.

You can drag an item from Launchpad to add it to the Dock. The app is in the Dock and in Launchpad.

Manage windows on Mac

When you open an app or the Finder on your Mac, a window opens on the desktop. Only one app at a time is active; the name of the app (in bold) and the app menus are shown in the menu bar.

Some apps, such as Safari or Mail, let you open multiple windows or different types of windows at the same time. MacOS provides several ways to manage open apps and windows.

Move, align, and merge windows

On your Mac, do any of the following:

- *Move a window:* Drag the window by its title bar to where you want it. Some windows can't be moved.

- *Align windows:* Drag a window close to another one—as the window nears the other one, it aligns without overlapping. You can position multiple windows adjacent to each other.

  To make adjacent windows the same size, drag the edge you want to resize—as it nears the edge of the adjacent window, it aligns with the edge and stops

  Drag the edge until it stops aligned with the edge of the adjacent window.

- Merge *an app's windows into one tabbed window:* In the app, choose Window > Merge All Windows.

To make a tab a separate window again, select the tab, then choose Window > Move Tab to New Window, or just drag the tab out of the window.

Maximize or minimize windows

On your Mac, do any of the following in a window:

- *Maximize a window:* Press and hold the Option key while you click the green maximize button ⊕ in the top-left corner of an app window. To return to the previous window size, Option-click the button again.

You can also double-click an app's title bar to maximize the window (as long as the option to do so is set to "zoom" in Dock preferences).

- *Minimize a window:* Click the yellow minimize button in the top-left corner of the window, or press Command-M.

You can set an option in Dock preferences to have a window minimize when you double-click its title bar.

Most windows can be manually resized. Drag the window's edge (top, bottom, or sides) or double-click an edge to expand that side of the window.

Quickly switch between app windows

On your Mac, do any of the following:

- *Switch to the previous app:* Press Command-Tab.
- *Scroll through all open apps:* Press and hold the Command key, press the Tab key, then press the Left or Right arrow key until you get to the app you want. Release the Command key.

If you change your mind while scrolling through the apps and don't want to switch apps, press Esc (Escape) or the Period key, then release the Command key.

Close a window

- In a window on your Mac, click the red close button ⊗ in the top-left corner of the window, or press Command-W.

If an app can have multiple windows open, such as Safari or Mail, closing a window does not close or quit the app. To quit these apps, click the app's name in the menu bar, then choose Quit [*App*]. You can hide or quit the active app by pressing Command-H or Command-Q.

You can use Mission Controlto quickly arrange open windows and spaces in a single layer to easily spot the one you need.

Use apps in full screen on Mac

On your Mac, move the pointer to the green button in the top-left corner of the window, then choose Enter Full Screen from the menu that appears or click the button.

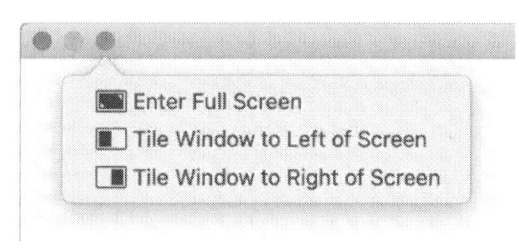

- In full screen, do any of the following:

- *Show or hide the menu bar:* Move the pointer to or away from the top of the screen.

- *Show or hide the Dock:* Move the pointer to or away from the Dock's location.

- *Move between other apps in full screen:* Swipe left or right on the trackpad.

- To stop using the app full screen, move the pointer to the green button again, then choose Exit Full Screen from the menu that appears or click the button .

To work in a bigger window without going full screen, maximize (or zoom) the window. Move the pointer to the green button in the top-left corner of the window, press and hold the Option key, then choose Zoom from the menu that appears or click the button . The window expands, but the menu bar and the Dock remain visible. To return to the previous window size, press and hold the Option key, then click the green button again.

You can also double-click an app's title bar to maximize the window. If the app minimizes into the Dock instead, change the title bar setting in Dock preferences.

If you're using an app full screen, you can quickly choose another app to use in Split View. Press Control-Up Arrow (or swipe up with three or four fingers) to enter Mission Control, then drag a window from Mission Control onto the thumbnail of the full-screen app in the Spaces bar. You can also drag one app thumbnail onto another in the Spaces bar.

Use apps in Split View on Mac

Many apps on your Mac support Split View mode, where you can work in two apps side by side at the same time.

On your Mac, move the pointer to the green button in the top-left corner of the window, then choose Tile Window to Left of Screen or Tile Window to Right of Screen from the menu that appears.

1. On the other side of the screen, click the second app you want to work with.
2. In Split View, do any of the following:
    - *Make one side bigger:* Move the pointer over the separator bar located in the middle, then drag it left or right. To return to the original sizes, double-click the separator bar.
    - *Change sides:* Use a window's toolbar to drag the window to the other side. If you don't see a

toolbar, click the window, then move the pointer to the top of the screen.

- *Show or hide the menu bar:* Move the pointer to or away from the top of the screen.
- *Show or hide the Dock:* Move the pointer to or away from the Dock's location.

3. To stop using an app in Split View, click its window, show the menu bar, move the pointer to the green button in the top-left corner of the window, then choose Exit Full Screen from the menu that appears or click the button .

The remaining app expands to full screen and can be accessed in the Spaces bar. To stop using the app full screen, move the pointer over its thumbnail in the Spaces bar, then click the Exit button that appears in the top-left corner of the thumbnail.

If you're using an app full screen, you can quickly choose another app to work with in Split View. Press Control-Up Arrow (or swipe up with three or four fingers) to enter Mission Control, then drag a window from Mission Control onto the thumbnail of the full-screen app in the Spaces bar. You can also drag one app thumbnail onto another in the Spaces bar.

Find, buy, and download apps in the App Store on Mac

To find the perfect app, search for it or browse the App Store. Once you find the app you want, you can purchase it using your Apple ID, or you can redeem a download code or a gift card.

To change your settings for downloads and purchases, choose Apple Menu > System Preferences > Apple ID, click Media & Purchases in the sidebar, then choose your options.

Find and buy apps

1. In the App Store on your Mac, do any of the following:
    - *Search for an app:* Enter one or more words in the search field at the top-left corner of the App Store window, then press Enter.
    - *Browse the App Store:* Click Discover, Create, Work, Play, Develop, or Categories in the sidebar on the left.
2. Click an app's name or icon to get a description and view customer ratings and reviews.
3. To download the app, click the button that shows the price of the app or "Get." Then click the button again to install or buy the app (or use Touch ID).

Change your settings for downloads and purchases

1. In the App Store on your Mac, choose Apple Menu > System Preferences.

2. Click Apple ID.

3. Click Media & Purchases (in the sidebar).

4. Choose your options.

Redeem iTunes gift cards, Apple Music cards, or a download code

- In the App Store on your Mac, click your name in the bottom-left corner (or click Sign In if you're not already), then click Redeem Gift Card in the top-right corner. Enter the download code or the code from your gift card.

  If you have a gift card with a box around the code, you can use the built-in camera on your Mac to redeem the card. After you click Redeem, click Use Camera, then hold the gift card 4 to 7 inches (10 to 18 centimeters) from the camera. Make sure the code area is near the center of the preview area, then hold the card steady until its redeemed.

Purchase in-app content and subscriptions

- Some apps sell extra content, including app upgrades, game content, and subscriptions. To make an in-app purchase, enter your Apple ID(or use Touch ID).

Download apps purchased by other family members

If you're part of a Family Sharing group, you can download eligible apps purchased by other family members.

1. In the App Store on your Mac, click your name in the bottom-left corner, or click Sign In if you're not already.

2. Click the "Purchased by" menu, then choose a family member.

3. Click the iCloud status icon next to an item to download it.

Install and reinstall apps purchased from the App Store on Mac

There are several ways to install and reinstall apps that you purchased with your Apple ID or that came with your new Mac.

Note: In the App Store, all of your purchases are tied to your Apple ID, and can't be transferred to another Apple ID. If you make purchases on your iPhone, iPad, or another Mac, always sign in using the same Apple ID so you can see all of your store purchases on this Mac and download any available updates.

Install apps that you purchased on a different computer

You can install and reinstall any app that you purchased with your Apple ID on other Mac computers.

- In the App Store on your Mac, click your name in the bottom-left corner, or click Sign In if you're not already, then click the redownload button.

Automatically download apps that you purchased on a different computer

1. In the App Store on your Mac, click your name in the bottom-left corner, or click Sign In if you're not already.

2. Choose App Store > Preferences, then select "Automatically download apps purchased on other Mac computers."

Reinstall apps

If you uninstalled or deleted an app that you purchased in the App Store, you can install it again.

- In the App Store on your Mac, click your name in the bottom-left corner, or click Sign In if you're not already, locate the app you want, then click the redownload button.

Manage subscriptions

You can view or change options for subscriptions you purchased in the App Store, the iTunes Store, or Apple News.

1. In the App Store on your Mac, click your name in the bottom-left corner, or click Sign In if you're not already.

   Make sure you sign in with the same Apple ID you used to purchase your subscriptions.

2. Click View Information, sign in again if necessary, and then click Manage (to the right of Subscriptions).

3. Click Edit (if you have more than one subscription), then do any of the following:

   - *Change subscription options:* In the Options list, select a setting, then click done.
   - *Cancel your subscription:* Click Cancel Subscription, confirm the cancellation, then click done.

Reinstall apps that came with your Mac

If an app is damaged or not working, you can try to reinstall it.

- To reinstall an app that came with macOS (for example, Music, Photos, Calendar, Safari, and more), reinstall macOS.

  Reinstalling macOS doesn't erase your information.

  If the apps came on a disc, and don't appear in the App Store, use the disc to reinstall them.

Install and uninstall apps from the internet or disc on Mac

You can download and install apps from the internet or a disc. If you no longer want an app, you can remove it.

Install apps

On your Mac, do any of the following:

- *For apps downloaded from the internet:* In the Downloads folder, double-click the disk image or package file (looks like an open box). If the provided installer doesn't open automatically, open it, then follow the onscreen instructions.

  Note: If you get a warning dialog about installing an app from an unidentified developer, *for apps on a disc:* Insert the disc into the optical drive on your Mac or connected to your Mac.

Uninstall apps

You can remove apps that you downloaded and installed from the internet or from a disc.

1. On your Mac, click the Finder icon in the Dock, then click Applications in the Finder sidebar.

2. Do one of the following:

    - If an app is in a folder, open the app's folder to check for an Uninstaller. If you see Uninstall [*App*] or [*App*] Uninstaller, double-click it, then follow the onscreen instructions.

- If an app isn't in a folder or doesn't have an Uninstaller, drag the app from the Applications folder to the Trash (at the end of the Dock).

WARNING: The app is permanently removed from your Mac the next time you or the Finder empties the Trash. If you have files that you created with the app, you may not be able to open them again. If you decide you want to keep the app, get it back before emptying the Trash—select the app in the Trash, then choose File > Put Back.

Chapter 6
Customize your Mac

Customize your Mac with System Preferences

You can change system settings to customize your Mac. For example, you can change the size and location of the Dock, choose a light or dark appearance, change the desktop picture, and more.

To change System Preferences on your Mac, click the System Preferences icon in the Dock or choose Apple menu > System Preferences.

Explore preferences

Options for your Mac are organized into preferences. For example, options you can set for Spotlight are located in Spotlight preferences.

Preferences appear as a grid of icons; the icons shown may vary depending on your Mac and the apps you have installed. Click an icon to open a preference pane and see the options.

By default, preferences are arranged in rows by category. To see them in alphabetical order, choose View > Organize Alphabetically.

Set options

Each preference pane contains options you can set. Most panes include a Help button ⓘ to click for more information about the options.

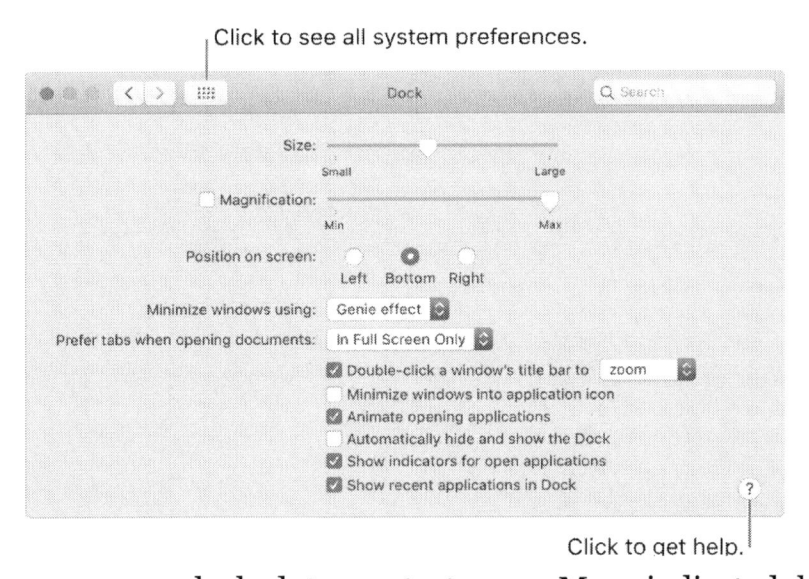

Click to see all system preferences.

Click to get help.

Some panes are locked to protect your Mac, indicated by a closed lock icon at the bottom of the pane, and the options are dimmed. To unlock a pane so you can set options, click the lock icon, and then enter the administrator password for your Mac.

Find options

If you don't know where to find an option in System Preferences, use the search field at the top of the window. Options that match your search text are listed, and the preference panes where they're located are highlighted.

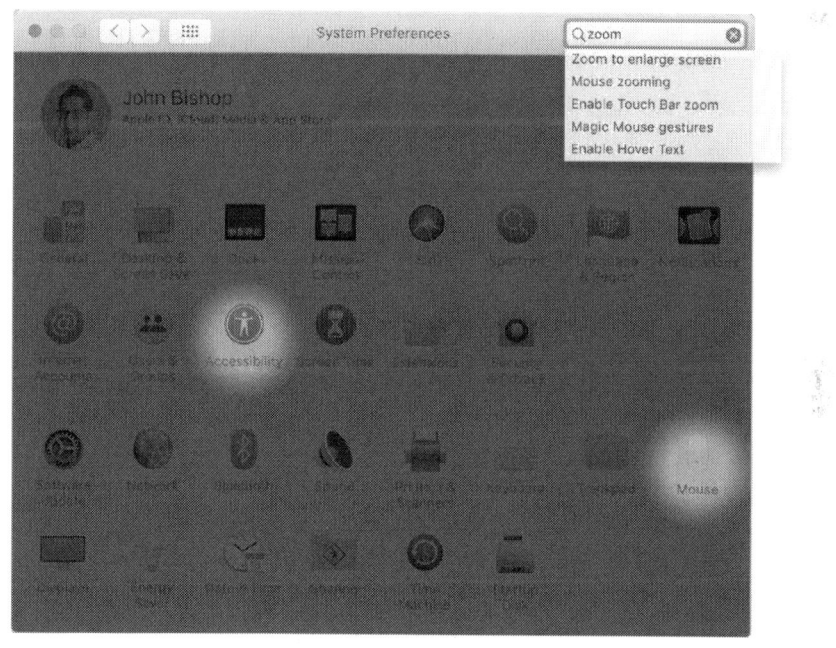

If you see a red badge on the System Preferences icon in the Dock, you need to take one or more actions. For example, if you didn't fully set up iCloud, the badge appears on the icon in the Dock; when you click the icon, the preferences are displayed so you can complete setup.

To change options for an app, such as Mail or Safari, open the app, click the app's name in the menu bar, and then choose Preferences.

Customize the desktop picture on your Mac

You can choose the picture that's displayed on your desktop. Your Mac comes with dozens of desktop pictures to choose from, or you can use your own pictures or choose a solid color.

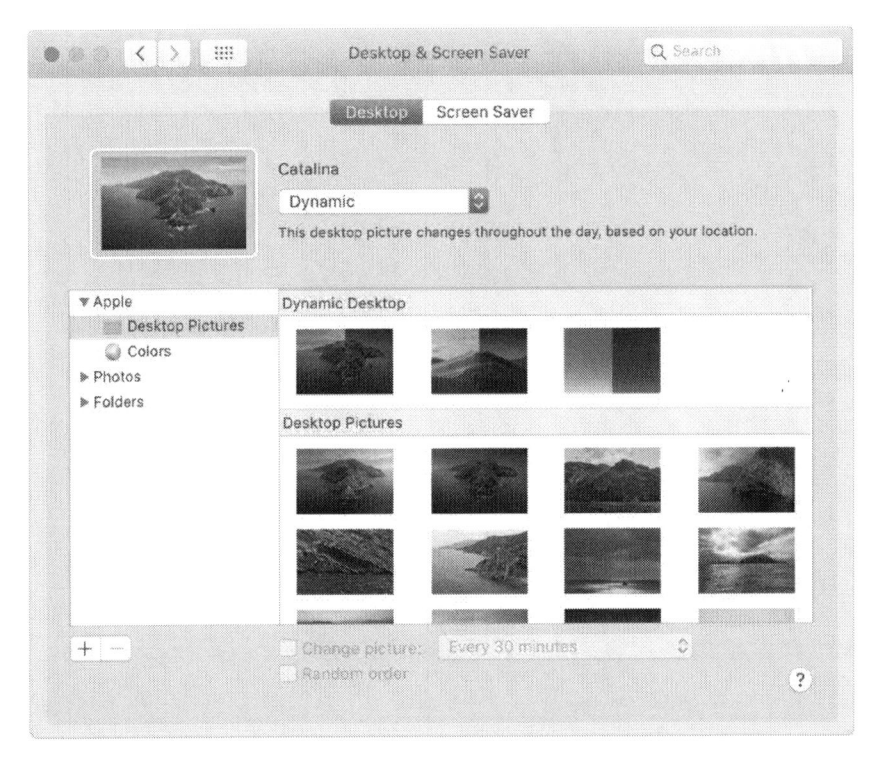

Tip: You can drag an image from your desktop or a folder onto the thumbnail at the top of the pane to use the image as your desktop picture.

1. On your Mac, choose Apple menu > System Preferences, click Desktop & Screen Saver, then click Desktop.

2. On the left, find a picture or color:

    o *Pictures and colors that come with your Mac:* Click the disclosure triangle next to Apple, then select Desktop Pictures or Colors to see thumbnails of available pictures and colors.

    Dynamic desktop pictures can automatically change throughout the course of the day based on your current location. If Location Services is turned off in Privacy preferences, the picture changes based on the time zone specified in Date & Time preferences.

    Some dynamic desktop pictures may also provide still images so the desktop picture doesn't distract from the light or dark appearance. For example, if you chose the dark appearance during macOS setup, the desktop picture is set to a dark still image. To use or stop using a still image (if available), click the pop-up menu, then choose an option.

- *Your pictures:* Click the disclosure triangle next to Photos (or iPhoto if available). If your pictures are in the Pictures or another folder, click the triangle next to Folders, then select a folder.

  To add a folder, click the Add button ＋, navigate to and select the folder, then click Choose.

  If you don't see anything when you select the folder that contains your pictures, they might not have the right file format—JPEG, PICT, TIFF, PNG, or HEIC. To change a picture's format, open it in the Preview app, then save it in the new format. If pictures look fuzzy, try using larger ones, such as 1024 x 768 pixels.

3. On the right, click the picture you want to use.

   The desktop immediately changes, so you can see how the picture looks. When you use one of your own pictures, you can choose to have it fill the screen, be centered, or otherwise arranged. It's easy to click around and try different pictures and arrangements until you find the one you like best.

   To use all the pictures in a folder, select the "Change picture" checkbox, then choose how often you want the picture to change—for example, every hour. The pictures are shown in the order they appear in the folder, or you can choose to show them in a random order.

To quickly use a picture you have in the Photos app, select the picture in Photos, click the Share button ⬆ in the Photos toolbar, then choose Set Desktop Picture.

You can use a picture you see on the web as your desktop picture. Control-click the image in the browser window, then select Use Image as Desktop Picture.

Use your internet accounts on Mac

You can use Exchange, Google, Yahoo, and other internet accounts in Mac apps by adding the accounts to your Mac.

You add internet accounts, and manage account settings, in Internet Accounts preferences. You can also add internet accounts from some apps that use them.

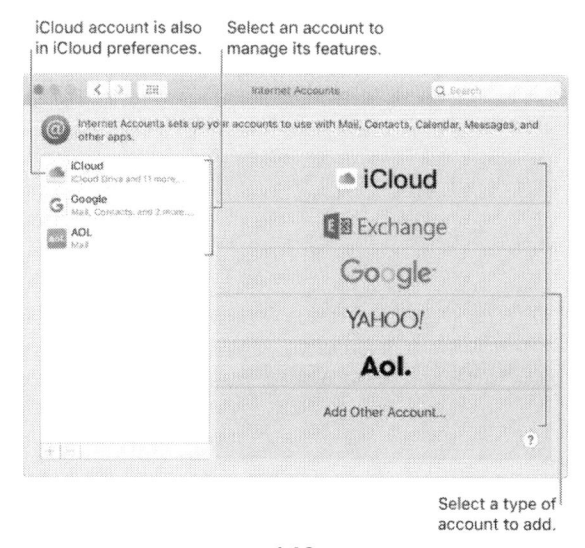

An iCloud account you add using the iCloud preferences in Apple ID preferences also appears in Internet Accounts preferences. You can change its settings in either place.

Add an account from an app

You can add accounts from Mail, Contacts, and Calendar. Accounts you add from the apps appear in Internet Accounts preferences.

1. In an app on your Mac, click the app menu, then choose Add account.

   For example, in Mail, choose Mail > Add account.

2. Select the account provider, then follow the onscreen instructions.

   If you want to add an account from a provider that isn't listed, such as a mail or calendar account for your company or school, click Other [*Type of*] Account, click Continue, then enter the requested account settings. If you don't know the account settings, ask the account provider.

Add an account in Internet Accounts preferences

Before you can add an account in Internet Accounts preferences, you must create the account on the provider's website.

1. On your Mac, choose Apple menu > System Preferences, then click Internet Accounts.

2. Click an account provider.

   If you don't yet have an account from a particular provider, such as Yahoo, create one on the provider's website, then add it here.

   If you want to add an account from a provider that isn't listed, such as a mail or calendar account for your company or school, click Add Other Account on the right, click the type of account you want to add, then enter the requested account settings. If you don't know the type of account or the account settings, ask the account provider.

3. Enter your account name, password, and other requested information, then click Set Up.

4. If the account you added has a list of features on the right, select the ones you want to use.

Change account features and details

1. On your Mac, choose Apple menu > System Preferences, then click Internet Accounts.

2. Select an account on the left, then do one of the following:

- *Turn features on or off:* Select each feature you want to use, and deselect any feature you don't want to use.

- *Change account details:* For the selected account, click Details on the right. Some accounts show the account name, a description, and other details on the right and don't have a Details button.

Stop using an account

1. On your Mac, choose Apple menu > System Preferences, then click Internet Accounts.

2. Select the account you want to stop using, then do one of the following:

   - *Remove the account and turn off its features:* Click the Remove button ―.

     If your Mac is set up for iCloud Keychain and you remove an account (other than your primary iCloud account), you're asked whether to remove the account from your other Mac computers set up for iCloud Keychain or just turn off all the account features on this Mac.

   - *Turn off a specific feature:* Deselect it.

Note: Deleting an account or turning off individual features can remove data stored in your apps. The data may be restored if you turn on the feature or add the account again. If you're not sure, ask the account provider.

Set up Screen Time for yourself on Mac

On your Mac, turn on Screen Time to learn how you spend time on your Mac and other devices. When Screen Time is turned on, you can view reports that show app usage, the number of notifications you receive, and how often you use your devices.

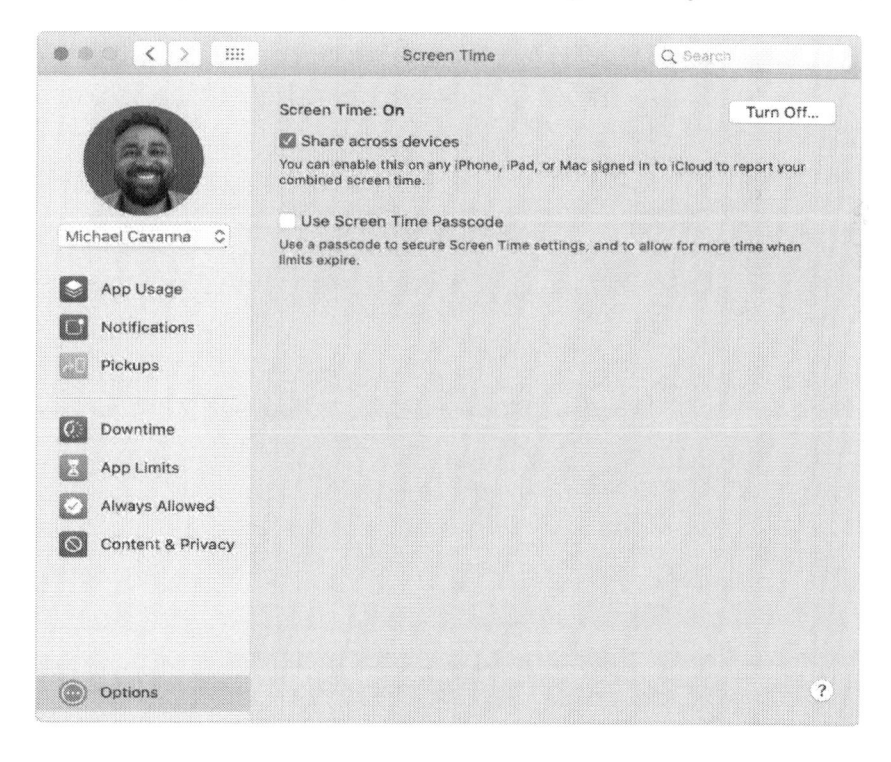

1. On your Mac, choose Apple menu > System Preferences, then click Screen Time .

2. If you're a member of a Family Sharing group, click the pop-up menu in the sidebar, then choose yourself.

    If you aren't using Family Sharing, you won't see a pop-up menu in the sidebar.

3. Click Options in the lower-left corner of the sidebar.

4. Click Turn On in the upper-right corner.

5. Select any of the following options:

    - *Share across devices:* Select this option if you want Screen Time reports to include time spent on other devices signed in with the same Apple ID.

        This option is available only when you're signed in with your Apple ID.

    - *Use Screen Time Passcode:* Select this option to secure Screen Time settings, and to require a passcode to allow additional time when limits expire.

6. If you want to, do any of the following:

    - Click Downtime in the sidebar, then set up a downtime schedule.

- Click App Limits in the sidebar, then set time limits for apps and websites.
- Click Always Allowed in the sidebar, then choose apps that can be used at any time.
- Click Content & Privacy in the sidebar, then set up content & privacy restrictions.

Change the appearance of the desktop

- *Make the desktop less transparent:* Choose Apple menu > System Preferences, click Accessibility, click Display, click Display, and then select "Reduce transparency." The transparent areas of the desktop and app windows become gray.

- *Choose a desktop picture with fewer colors or shapes:* Choose Apple menu > System Preferences, click Desktop & Screen Saver, click Desktop, browse through the picture folders on the left, then select a less busy picture or a solid color on the right.

- *Make borders darker:* Choose Apple menu > System Preferences, click Accessibility, click Display, click Display, then select "Increase contrast." macOS automatically reduces transparency and makes the borders of buttons, boxes, and other items on the screen more visible.

- *Use a dark appearance:* Choose Apple menu > System Preferences, click General, then click the Dark appearance. You can change the accent and highlight colors.

- *Invert colors:* Choose Apple menu > System Preferences, click Accessibility, click Display, click Display, and then select "Invert colors." If you turn on Night Shift, "Invert colors" is automatically disabled.

- *Make colors easier on your eyes at night:* Use NightShift to make the colors on the screen warmer.

- *Differentiate or tone down colors:* Apply color filtersor tint the entire screen.

- *Make the pointer bigger:* Choose Apple menu > System Preferences, click Accessibility, click Display, click Cursor, then drag the Cursor Size slider to the right as far as you need.

Tip: If you lose track of the pointer on the screen, quickly move your finger on the trackpad or quickly move the mouse—the pointer briefly gets bigger so you can see it. To turn this feature off, choose Apple menu > System Preferences, click Accessibility, click Display, click Cursor, then deselect "Shake mouse pointer to locate."

Make text bigger

- *Increase the text size of emails in Mail:* In Mail, choose Mail > Preferences, click Fonts & Colors, click Select next to "Message font," then select a font size in the Fonts window.

- *Increase the text size of messages in Messages:* In Messages, choose Messages > Preferences, click General, then move the "Text size" slider to the right.

- *Increase the text size in other apps:* In many apps, you can press Command-Plus (+) or Command-Minus (–) to adjust text size. If that doesn't work, check the app's preferences.

Make icons and other items bigger

- *Increase the size of icons and text on the desktop:* Control-click the desktop, choose Show View Options, then move the "Icon size" slider to the right. Click the "Text size" pop-up menu, then choose a text size.

- *Increase the size of icons and text in the Finder:* Select an item in the Finder, then choose View > Show View Options. The view you're using determines how you increase the size.

- o *Icon view:* Move the "Icon size" slider to the right. Click the "Text size" pop-up menu, then choose a text size.
- o *List view:* Select the larger icon size to the right of "Icon size." Click the "Text size" pop-up menu, then choose a text size.
- o *Column view:* Click the "Text size" pop-up menu, then choose a text size. You can't choose an icon size.
- o *Gallery view:* Select the largest thumbnail size. You can't choose a text size.

- *Increase the size of items in the Finder and Mail sidebars:* Choose Apple menu > System Preferences, click General, click the "Sidebar icon size" pop-up menu, then choose Large.

Use zoom

- *Zoom in on the screen:* Choose Apple menu > System Preferences, click Accessibility, then click Zoom. You can zoom the entire screen or an area of it.
  - o When "Use keyboard shortcuts to zoom" is selected, you can zoom in (press Option-Command-Equal sign), zoom out (press Option-Command-

Minus sign), or quickly switch between the two settings (press Option-Command-8).

- When "Use scroll gesture with modifier keys to zoom" is selected, you can zoom in by pressing and holding the Control key (or another modifier key) and swiping up with two fingers on your trackpad.

- *Zoom in on the item under the pointer:* Choose Apple menu > System Preferences, click Accessibility, click Zoom, and then select Enable Hover Text. *Zoom in on webpages:* In Safari, choose View > Zoom In, or press Command-Plus (+). You can choose Zoom In or press Command-Plus multiple times to continue zooming in. If you want to zoom just the text and not images, choose Zoom Text Only.

- *Zoom in on PDFs, images, and webpages:* If your mouse or trackpad supports it, you can zoom in or out using a simple gesture. Choose Apple menu > System Preferences, click Mouse > Point & Click or Trackpad > Scroll & Zoom, then select Smart zoom. Now to zoom in or out, double-tap on your mouse with one finger or on your trackpad with two fingers.

Use accessibility features on Mac

Accessibility comes standard with a Mac. Whether you have difficulties with vision, hearing, or physical mobility, macOS includes a variety of features to help you work in alternative ways—and make your Mac even easier to use.

Use the built-in screen reader called Voiceover

Voiceover is the built-in screen reader that describes aloud what appears on your screen and speaks the text in documents, webpages, and windows. Using Voiceover, you control your Mac with the keyboard or trackpad gestures. You can also connect a refreshable braille display to use with Voiceover.

- To turn Voiceover on or off, press Command-F5 (or if your Mac has Touch ID, press and hold the Command key, then quickly press Touch ID three times).

- To customize Voiceover using Voiceover Utility, press Control-Option-F8 (when Voiceover is on).

- To learn how to use Voiceover, choose Apple menu > System Preferences, click Accessibility, click Voiceover, and then click Open Voiceover Training.

For help with Voiceover, choose Help > Voiceover Help while Voiceover Utility is open.

Make content on the screen larger

- You can use your mouse or use your trackpad to zoom and make the entire screen larger or just an area of it. If you're using a second display with your Mac, you can choose which display to zoom—or zoom both.

- You can use Hover Text to zoom whatever is under the pointer—text, fields, menu items, buttons, and more—in high resolution in a separate window.

Reduce motion on the screen

If motion on the screen of your Mac is problematic, you can set an option to reduce motion when using certain features, such as Spaces, Notification Center, or the Dock.

1. Choose Apple menu > System Preferences, click Accessibility, click Display, and then click Display.
2. Select Reduce motion.

Use a physical keyboard or an onscreen keyboard

Set options that make it easier to press keys on a physical keyboard, or bypass a physical keyboard altogether and use the onscreen Accessibility Keyboard instead.

1. Choose Apple menu > System Preferences, click Accessibility, then click Keyboard.
2. Do any of the following:

- Click Hardware, then turn on Sticky Keys and Slow Keys.
- Click Accessibility Keyboard, then turn on the Accessibility Keyboard.

Control the pointer and mouse actions using alternate methods

- When you enable Mouse Keys, you can use the keyboard or a numeric keypad to control the pointer.
- When you enable Alternate Pointer Actions, you can use keyboard shortcuts or assistive switches to perform mouse actions, such as left, right, or double clicks.

To enable these options, choose Apple menu > System Preferences, click Accessibility, click Pointer Control, and then click Alternate Control Methods.

Use Voice Control and text to speech

- With Voice Control, you can use spoken commands to open apps, choose menu items, and more on your Mac. MacOS provides a standard set of commands, and you can create your own commands. You can have your Mac speak the text in dialogs and alert messages, and notify you when an app needs you to do something, such as accept a Messages invitation.

Change how your keyboard, mouse, and trackpad work

You can set various options to customize how your keyboard, mouse, and trackpad work while using your Mac. For example, you can adjust the speed at which the pointer moves across the screen when you move your finger across the trackpad.

- To set options for your keyboard, choose Apple menu > System Preferences, then click Keyboard.

- To set options for your mouse, choose Apple menu > System Preferences, then click Mouse.

- To set options for your trackpad, including gestures, choose Apple menu > System Preferences, then click Trackpad.

Control your Mac with assistive devices

- With Switch Control, you can use one or more adaptive accessories to enter text, interact with items on the screen, and control your Mac. Switch Control scans a panel or user interface until a switch is used to select an item or perform an action.

   Use Switch Control

- When you use the Accessibility Keyboard, you can use Dwell with a tracking device to control the pointer so it's easier to enter text, interact with items on the screen, and control your Mac. With Dwell, you can dwell for a specified amount of time on a control to perform a mouse action.

Control the pointer using Dwell

You can easily check which accessibility features are on, right from the menu bar: select the checkbox at the bottom of Accessibility preferences to show accessibility status in the menu bar.

You can use the Accessibility Options shortcut panel to quickly turn some options on or off. To select the options that are included in the panel, choose Apple menu > System Preferences, click Accessibility, then click Shortcut.

In some apps, you can have your Mac speak text by choosing Edit > Speech > Start Speaking. This functionality might not be available for all languages.

Change people's pictures in apps on Mac

You can add or change your picture shown in the login window and in various apps on your Mac, and choose pictures to use for your friends, family, and other contacts.

See pictures for your contacts in Messages

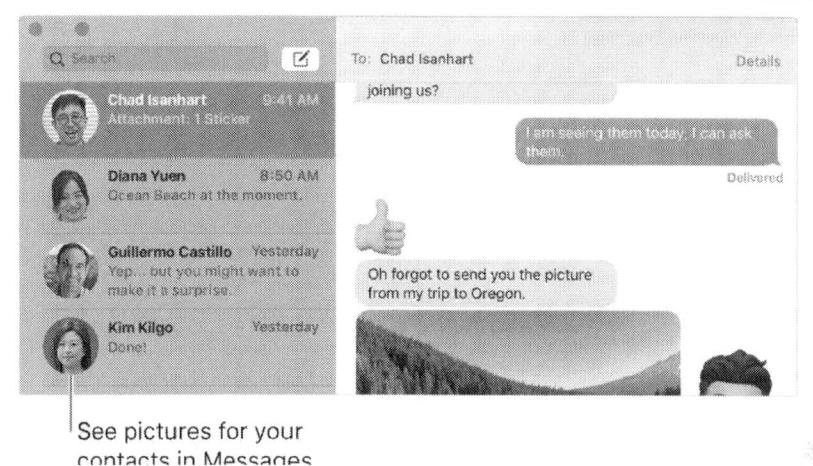

Your user picture

Change the picture that appears next to your name or another user's name in the login window.

Your picture in Messages

Other people see the picture they have stored for you in their Contacts app, and you see the picture you have stored for them in your Contacts. If a picture isn't available, a monogram is shown.

Your picture in Mail

Mail can show a picture for you and for people who email you, depending on the pictures that are available in the Contacts app. The pictures are shown only to you; they aren't included in your emails.

Pictures in Contacts

Include your picture in your contact card. You can also use pictures of people in their contact cards (the pictures may appear in other apps). Your contacts don't see the pictures you choose—only you do.

Set up users, guests, and groups on Mac

If your Mac has multiple users, you should set up an account for each person so each can personalize settings and options without affecting the others. You can let occasional users log in as guests without access to other users' files or settings. You can also create groups. You must be an administrator of your Mac to perform these tasks.

Add a user

1. On your Mac, choose Apple menu > System Preferences, then click Users & Groups.

2. Click the lock icon to unlock it.

3. Enter an administrator name and password.

4. Click the Add button below the list of users.

5. Click the New Account pop-up menu, then choose a type of user.

    - *Administrator:* An administrator can add and manage other users, install apps, and change settings. The new user you create when you first set up your Mac is an administrator. Your Mac can have multiple administrators. You can create new ones, and convert standard users to administrators. Don't set up automatic login for an administrator. If you do, someone could simply restart your Mac and gain access with administrator privileges. To keep your Mac secure, don't share administrator names and passwords.

- *Standard:* Standard users are set up by an administrator. Standard users can install apps and change their own settings, but can't add other users or change other users' settings.

- *Sharing Only:* Sharing-only users can access shared files remotely, but can't log in to or change settings on the computer. To give the user permission to access your shared files or screen, you may need to change settings in the File Sharing, Screen Sharing, or Remote Management pane of sharing preferences. See Set up file sharing and Share the screen of another Mac.

For more information about the options for each type of user, click the Help button in the lower-left corner of the dialog.

6. Enter a full name for the new user. An account name is generated automatically. To use a different account name, enter it now—you can't change it later.

7. Enter a password for the user, then enter it again to verify. Enter a password hint to help the user remember their password.

8. Click Create User.

9. Depending on the type of user you create, you can also do any of the following:

    o For an administrator, select "Allow user to administer this computer."

    o Use Sharing preferences to specify whether the user can share your files and share your screen.

For information about Apple's privacy policy,

If your Mac has Touch ID, a new user can add a fingerprint after logging in to the Mac. The user can then use Touch ID to unlock the Mac and password-protected items, and purchase items from the iTunes Store, App Store, and Apple Books using their Apple ID.

Create a group

A group allows multiple users to have the same access privileges. For example, you can grant a group specific access privileges for a folder or a file, and all members of the group have access. You can also assign a group specific access privileges for each of your shared folders.

1. On your Mac, choose Apple menu > System Preferences, then click Users & Groups.

2. Click the lock icon to unlock it.

3. Enter an administratorname and password.

4. Click the Add button below the list of users.

5. Click the New Account pop-up menu, then choose Group.

6. Give the group a name, then click Create Group.

7. Select each user and group you want to add to the new group.

Use Sharing preferences to specify whether the group members can share your filesand share your screen.

Convert a standard user to an administrator

1. On your Mac, choose Apple menu > System Preferences, then click Users & Groups.

2. Click the lock icon to unlock it.

3. Enter an administrator name and password.

4. Select a standard user or managed user in the list of users, then select "Allow user to administer this computer."

Let occasional users log in as guests

You can let other people use your Mac temporarily as guest users without adding them as individual users.

- Guests don't need a password to log in.
- Guests can't change user or computer settings.
- Guests can't log in remotely when remote login is turned on in Sharing preferences.

Files created by a guest are stored in a temporary folder, but that folder and its contents are deleted when the guest logs out.

Guest access works with the Find My app to help you find your Mac if you lose it. You can locate your Mac if someone finds it, logs in as a guest, and then uses Safari to access the internet.

Note: If File Vault is turned on, guests can access Safari, but can't access your encrypted disk or create files.

1. On your Mac, choose Apple menu > System Preferences, then click Users & Groups.
2. Click the lock icon to unlock it.
3. Enter an administrator name and password.

4. Select Guest User in the list of users.

5. Select "Allow guests to log in to this computer."

6. If you like, select "Limit Adult Websites" to prevent the guest from accessing adult websites.

7. To let guests use your shared folders from another computer on the network, select "Allow guest users to connect to shared folders."

Customize the login experience

If you are an administrator, you can specify how the login window looks to all the other users.

1. On your Mac, choose Apple menu > System Preferences, click Users & Groups, then click Login Options.

2. Click the lock icon to unlock it.

3. Enter an administrator name and password.

4. Click the "Automatic login" pop-up menu, then choose a user, or choose off.

   If you choose a user, then whenever the Mac starts up, that user is automatically logged in. If you choose off, then at startup the Mac opens a login window showing all the users. Automatic login takes effect the next time you restart the Mac.

Note: Automatic login allows anyone to access your Mac simply by restarting it. If automatic login is enabled, make sure your Mac doesn't automatically log in an administrator. When File Vault is turned on, automatic login is disabled.

5. Select the options you want. If you have any questions, click the Help button ⓘ for detailed information.

To permit new users to access your shared files or screen, you may need to change settings in the File Sharing, Screen Sharing, or Remote Management pane of sharing preferences. See Set up file sharing and Share the screen of another Mac.

To open Sharing preferences, choose Apple menu > System Preferences, then click Sharing.

Run Windows on your Mac

Use Boot Camp to install and use Windows on your Mac.

Boot Camp Assistant helps you set up a Windows partition on your computer's hard disk and then start the installation of your Windows software.

After installing Windows and the Boot Camp drivers, you can start up your Mac in either Windows or macOS.

Chapter 7
Work with Files and Folders
Create and work with documents on Mac

You can use macOS apps—such as Pages or Text Edit—or apps from the Mac App Store to create reports, essays, spreadsheets, financial charts, presentations, slideshows, and more.

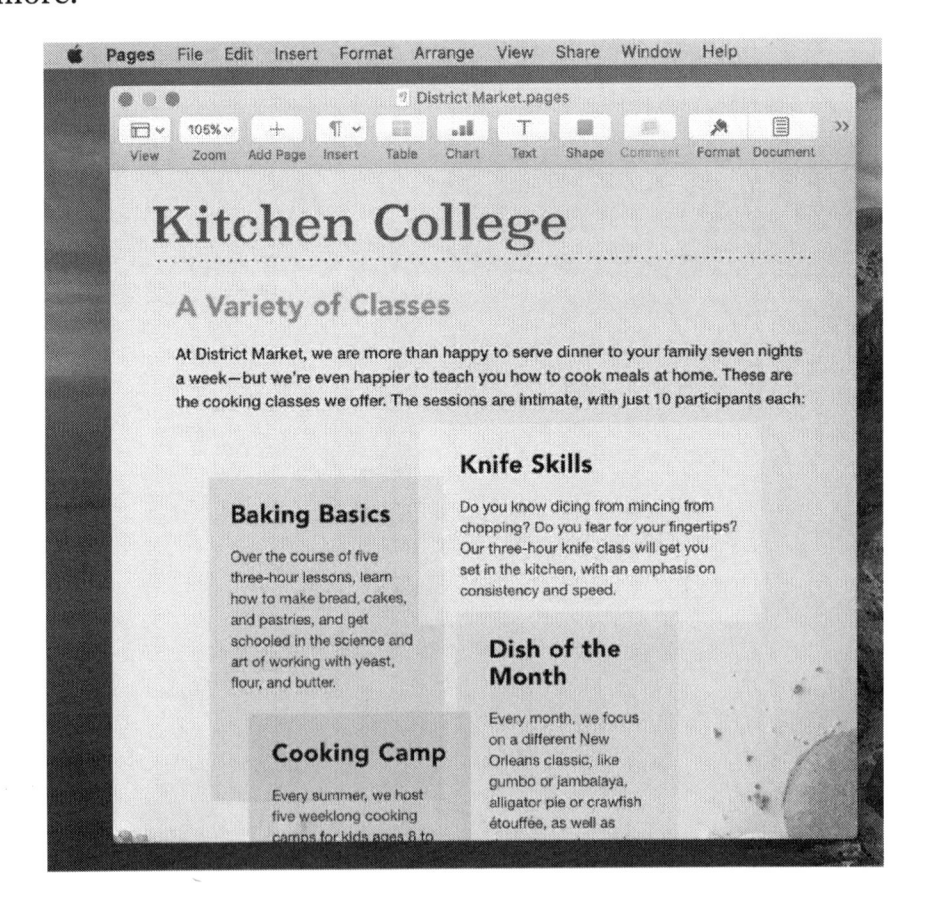

Create documents

1. On your Mac, open an app that lets you create documents.

   For example, open Text Edit to create a plain text, rich text, or HTML document.

2. Click New Document in the Open dialog, or choose File > New.

Many Mac computers come with these Apple apps that you can use to create spreadsheets, presentations, reports, and more.

- *Pages:* Create letters, reports, flyers, posters, and more. Pages includes many templates that make it easy to create beautiful documents.

- *Numbers:* Create spreadsheets to organize and present your data. Start with a template, then modify it however you like—add formulas, charts, images, and more.

- *Keynote:* Create compelling presentations with images, media, charts, slide animations, and more.

If you don't have Pages, Numbers, or Keynote on your Mac, you can get them from the App Store.

They're also available for your iOS and iPadOS devices (from the App Store) and on iCloud.com.

Format documents

There are several ways to format and work with text in documents on your Mac:

- *Change fonts and styles:* In a document, choose Format > Show Fonts or Format > Font > Show Fonts, or Format > Style.

- *Change colors:* In a document, choose Format > Show Colors, or Format > Font > Show Colors. *Enter different types of characters:* You can enter characters with accent marks or diacritic marks.

- *Check spelling:* In most apps, spelling is checked while you type, and mistakes are automatically corrected. You can turn off these features or use other options.

An app may provide additional ways to format and work with text, and with images and objects. To learn more about an app, choose Help in the menu bar while working in the app.

Save documents

Many apps on your Mac save your documents automatically (a feature known as *Auto Save*) while you work. You can save a document at any time.

- *Save a document:* In a document, choose File > Save, enter a name, choose where to save the document (to see more locations, click the down arrow button ⌄), then click Save.

When you save your document, you can add tags to help you find it later. You may be able to save your document in iCloud Drive so it's available on your computers and iOS and iPadOS devices set up with iCloud Drive.

- *Save a document with another name:* In a document, choose File > Save As, then enter a new name. If you don't see Save As, press and hold the Option key, then open the File menu again.

- *Save a document as a copy:* In a document, choose File > Duplicate or File > Save As.

You can also save a document as a PDF and combine multiple files into a single PDF.

Find documents

There are several ways to find documents on your Mac:

- *Use Spotlight:* Click the Spotlight icon in the menu bar, then enter the name of your document. You can also use Spotlight to specify criteria to narrow the search results.

- *Use tags:* If you tagged your document, click the Finder icon in the Dock to open a Finder window, then click the tag in the Finder sidebar.

- *Use the Recents folder:* In the sidebar of a Finder window, click Recents.

- *Use the Recent Items menu:* If you worked on a document recently, choose Apple menu > Recent Items.

In some apps, you can open recent documents by choosing File > Open Recent, then the document.

Dictate your messages and documents on Mac

With keyboard dictation, you can dictate text anywhere you can type it. Turn it on in the Dictation pane of Keyboard preferences to enable keyboard dictation—where your words are sent to Apple servers to be analyzed using the latest language data and converted into text in real-time. A feedback window gauges your speaking volume and provides basic dictation controls.

If you need to dictate text and control your Mac using your voice instead of a keyboard and trackpad, use Voice Control.

Note: When Voice Control is on, you can't use keyboard dictation.

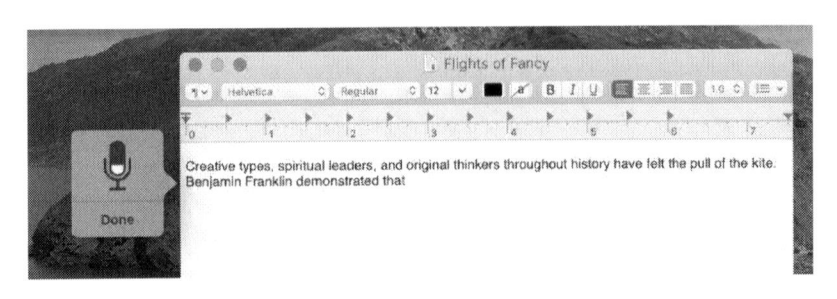

Turn on keyboard dictation

1. On your Mac, choose Apple menu > System Preferences, click Keyboard, then click Dictation.

2. Click On. If a prompt appears, click Enable Dictation.

3. To dictate using another language, click the Language pop-up menu, then choose your language and dialect.

   - *Add an unlisted language:* Choose Customize or Add Language, then select the languages you want to use.

   - *Remove a language:* Click the Language pop-up menu, choose Customize, and then deselect the language you don't want to use.

Dictate text

1. In an app on your Mac, place the insertion point where you want the dictated text to appear.

2. Press the dictation keyboard shortcut or choose Edit > Start Dictation.

3. When the feedback window shows a microphone icon with a fluctuating loudness indicator, or you hear the tone that signals your Mac is ready for keyboard dictation, dictate your text.

To insert a punctuation mark, such as a period or comma, say the name of the punctuation mark. You can also perform simple formatting tasks. For example, say "new line" or "new paragraph" to insert space between lines. For a list of the commands you can use while dictating, if you set up keyboard dictation for multiple languages and want to switch languages as you dictate, click the language in the feedback window, then choose the language you want.

For information about setting up keyboard dictation for multiple languages, see "Turn on keyboard dictation," above.

4. When you're done, press the dictation keyboard shortcut or click done in the feedback window.

Ambiguous text is underlined in blue. If the text is wrong, click it and select an alternate. You can also type or dictate the correct text.

Set a different keyboard dictation shortcut

By default, you press the FN (Function) key twice to start or stop keyboard dictation. If you like, you can choose a different dictation keyboard shortcut.

1. On your Mac, choose Apple menu > System Preferences, click Keyboard, then click Dictation.

2. Click the Shortcut pop-up menu, then choose a different shortcut.

   To create a shortcut that's not in the list, choose Customize, then press the keys you want to use. For example, you could press Option-Z.

Change the microphone used for keyboard dictation

The pop-up menu below the microphone icon in the Dictation pane of Keyboard preferences shows which device your Mac is currently using to listen.

1. On your Mac, choose Apple menu > System Preferences, click Keyboard, then click Dictation.

2. Click the pop-up menu below the microphone icon, then choose the microphone you want to use for keyboard dictation.

   If you choose Automatic, your Mac listens to the device you're most likely to use for keyboard dictation.

Turn off keyboard dictation

- On your Mac, choose Apple menu > System Preferences, click Keyboard, click Dictation, and then click Off.

Take screenshots or screen recordings on Mac

You can take pictures (called *screenshots*) or recordings of the screen on your Mac using Screenshot or keyboard shortcuts. Screenshot provides a panel of tools that let you easily take screenshots and screen recordings, with options to control what you capture—for example, you can set a timer delay or include the pointer or clicks.

Take pictures or screen recordings using Screenshot

1. On your Mac, press Shift-Command-5 (or use Launchpad) to open Screenshot and display the tools.

2. Click a tool to use to select what you want to capture or record (or use the Touch Bar).

   For a portion of the screen, drag the frame to reposition it or drag its edges to adjust the size of the area you want to capture or record.

3. Click Options if you want.

   The available options vary based on whether you're taking a screenshot or a screen recording. For example, you can choose to set a timed delay or show the mouse pointer or clicks, and specify where to save the file.

   The Show Floating Thumbnail option helps you work more easily with a completed shot or recording—it floats in the bottom-right corner of the screen for a few seconds so you have time to drag it into a document, mark it up, or share it before it's saved to the location you specified.

4. Start the screenshot or screen recording:

    - *For the entire screen or a portion of it:* Click Capture.

    - *For a window:* Move the cursor to the window, then click the window.

    - *For recordings:* Click Record. To stop recording, click the Stop Recording button ⏺ in the menu bar.

When the Show Floating Thumbnail option is set, you can do any of the following while the thumbnail is briefly displayed in the bottom-right corner of the screen:

- Swipe right to immediately save the file and make it disappear.

- Drag the thumbnail into a document, an email, a note, or a Finder window.

- Click the thumbnail to open a window where you can mark up the screenshot or trim the recording, or share it.

Depending on where you chose to save the screenshot or recording, an app may open.

Take pictures using keyboard shortcuts

You can use various keyboard shortcuts on your Mac to take pictures of the screen. The files are saved to the desktop.

Tip: To copy a screenshot so you can paste it somewhere—like in an email or to another device—press and hold the Control key while you press the other keys. For example, to copy the whole screen, press Shift-Command-Control-3.

Action	Shortcut
Capture the entire screen	Press Shift-Command-3.
Capture a portion of the screen	Press Shift-Command-4, then move the crosshair pointer to where you want to start the screenshot. Press the mouse or trackpad button, drag over the area you want to capture, then release the mouse or trackpad button.
Capture a	Press Shift-Command-4, then press

Action	Shortcut
window or the menu bar	the Space bar. Move the camera pointer over the window or the menu bar to highlight it, then click.
Capture a menu and menu items	Open the menu, press Shift-Command-4, and then drag the pointer over the menu items you want to capture.
Open Screenshot	Press Shift-Command 5.
Capture the Touch Bar	Press Shift-Command-6.

You can customize these keyboard shortcuts in the Shortcuts pane of Keyboard preferences. On your Mac, choose Apple menu > System Preferences, click Keyboard, then click Shortcuts.

Screenshots are saved as .png files and screen recordings are saved as .move files. Filenames begin with "Screen Shot" or "Screen Recording" and include the date and time.

You may not be able to take pictures of windows in some apps, such as DVD Player.

View and edit files with Quick Look on Mac

Quick Look offers a fast, full-size preview of nearly any kind of file without opening the file. Just press the Space bar to rotate photos, trim audio and video clips, and use Markup to crop photos and annotate images or PDFs. You can use Quick Look for items in Finder windows, on your desktop, in emails and messages, and other places.

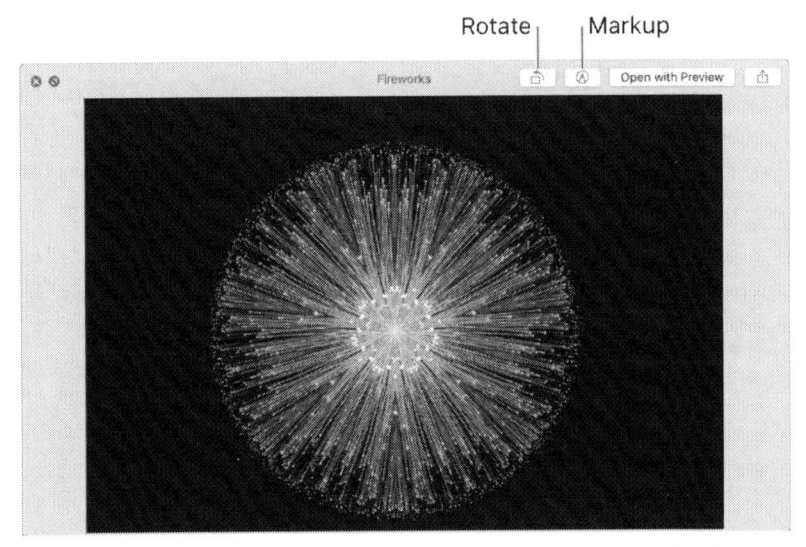

1. On your Mac in a Finder window or on the desktop, select one or more items, then press the Space bar.

   A Quick Look window opens. If you selected multiple items, the first item is shown.

2. In the Quick Look window, do any of the following:

   - *Resize the window:* Drag the corners of the window.

You can also use Quick Look full screen. Click the Full Screen button ⊘ in the Quick Look window. To stop using it full screen, move the pointer to the bottom of the window, then click the Exit Full Screen button ↙ that appears.

- *Browse items (if you selected multiple items):* Click the arrows near the top-left of the window or press the Left Arrow and Right Arrow keys. In full screen, click the Play button ▶ to view the items as a slideshow.

- *Show items in a grid (if you selected multiple items):* Click the Index Sheet button ▦ or press Command-Return.

- *Zoom in and out of an item:* Press Command-Plus (+) to make the image bigger or Command-Minus (–) to make it smaller.

- *Rotate an item:* Click the Rotate Left ↺ button or press and hold the Option key, then click the Rotate Right ↻ button. Keep clicking to continue rotating the item.

- *Mark up an item:* Click the Markup button Ⓐ.

- *Trim an audio or video item:* Click the Trim button, then drag the yellow handles in the trimming bar. To test your changes, click Play. You can start over by clicking Revert. When you're ready to save your changes, click done, then choose to replace the original file or create a new one.

- *Open an item:* Click Open with [*App*].

- *Share an item:* Click the Share button.

3. When you're done, press the Space bar or click the Close button to close the Quick Look window.

When you open a Live Photo in the Quick Look window, the video portion of the photo plays automatically. To view it again, click Live Photo in the bottom-left corner of the photo.

Mark up files on Mac

Markup on your Mac lets you write, sign, and draw on, or crop or rotate, PDF documents and images. If your iPhone or iPad is nearby, you can use Continuity Markup to mark up the file on your device—even using Apple Pencil on iPad—and instantly see the changes on your Mac.

To use Continuity features, your devices must meet system requirements. See the Apple Support article System requirements for Continuity on Mac, iPhone, iPad, iPod touch, and Apple Watch.

1. When using Quick Look on your Mac, click the Markup tool Ⓐ. Or when using Quick Actions, choose Markup.

   Markup is also available in various apps, such as Mail, Notes, Text Edit, and Photos.

2. Use the tools to mark up an image or a PDF document on your Mac; the tools that are available vary depending on the type of file.

   If your iPhone or iPad is nearby, click the Annotate tool to use Continuity Markup to mark up the file on your device. For information about using Apple Pencil on iPad, to switch between your markup and the iPad

Home screen, swipe up from the bottom of your iPad with one finger. To return to your markup, swipe up from the bottom with one finger to show the iPad Dock, then tap the Sidecar icon .

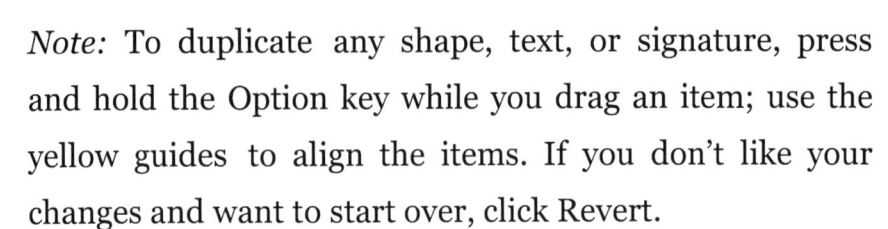

Note: To duplicate any shape, text, or signature, press and hold the Option key while you drag an item; use the yellow guides to align the items. If you don't like your changes and want to start over, click Revert.

Tool	Description
Sketch	Sketch a hape using a single stroke. If your drawing is recognized as a standard shape, it's replaced by that shape; to use your drawing instead, choose it from the palette that's shown.
Draw	Draw a shape using a single stroke. Press your finger more firmly on the trackpad to draw with a heavier, darker line. This tool appears only on computers with a Force Touch trackpad.
Shapes	Click a shape, then drag it where you want. To resize the shape, use the blue

181

Tool	Description
	handles. If it has green handles, use them to alter the shape. You can zoom and highlight shapes using these tools: • *Loupe* : Drag the loupe to the area you want to magnify. To increase or decrease the magnification, drag the green handle; drag the blue handle to change the loupe size. To further magnify an area, you can create additional loupes and stack them, using the yellow guides to align them. • *Highlight* : Drag the highlight where you want. To resize it, use the blue handles.
Text	Type your text, then drag the text box where you want.
Highlight	Highlight selected text.

Tool	Description
Selection	
Sign	If signatures are listed, click one, then drag it where you want. To resize it, use the blue handles. To create a new signature, click the Sign tool, click Create Signature if shown, then click how you want to create your signature: • *Use a trackpad:* Click Trackpad, click the text when asked, sign your name on the trackpad using your finger, and then click done. If you don't like the results, click Clear, then try again. If your trackpad supports it, press your finger more firmly on the trackpad to sign with a heavier, darker line. • *Use your Mac computer's built-*

Tool	Description
	in camera: Click Camera, hold your signature (on white paper) facing the camera so that your signature is level with the blue line in the window. When your signature appears in the window, click done. If you don't like the results, click Clear, then try again.
	• *Use your iPhone or iPad:* Click Select Device, then choose a device (if more than one is available). On your device, use your finger or Apple Pencil (on iPad) to sign your name, then click done. If you don't like the results, click Clear, then try again.
Shape Style	Change the thickness and type of lines used in a shape, and add a shadow.
Border Color	Change the color of the lines used in a shape.

Tool	Description
Fill Color	Change the color that's used inside a shape.
Text Style **A**	Change the font or the font style and color.
Rotate Left or Rotate Right	Click to rotate the item to the left. Continue clicking to keep rotating. To rotate the item to the right, press and hold the Option key, then click until you're done rotating the item.
Crop	Hide part of an item. Drag the corner handles until just the area you want to keep is shown within the frame's border. You can also drag the frame to reposition it. When you're ready, click Crop.
Annotate	Annotate the item using Continuity Markup to sketch or draw on it using your nearby iPhone or iPad.

Tool	Description
	The Annotate tool appears blue when your device is connected; to disconnect your device, click the tool again.

3. When you're finished with your markup, click done.

   If you're working in the Quick Look or Quick Actions window, your changes can't be undone after you close the window.

Combine files into a PDF on Mac

You can quickly combine multiple files into a PDF right from your desktop or a Finder window.

1. On you Mac, click the Finder icon in the Dock to open a Finder window.

2. Select the files you want to combine into a PDF.

   Alternatively, you can select the files on your desktop.

   Note: The files appear in the PDF in the same order that you select them.

3. Control-click the selected files, then choose Quick Actions > Create PDF.

The file is created automatically with a name similar to the first file you selected.

Tip: You can also select the files in the Finder and use the Create PDF button in the Preview pane of a Finder window. If you don't see the Preview pane on the right, choose View > Show Preview.

Print documents from your Mac

1. With a document open on your Mac, choose File > Print, or press Command-P.

   The Print dialog opens, with a small preview of how your document will look when printed. Click the arrows below the preview to scroll through the pages.

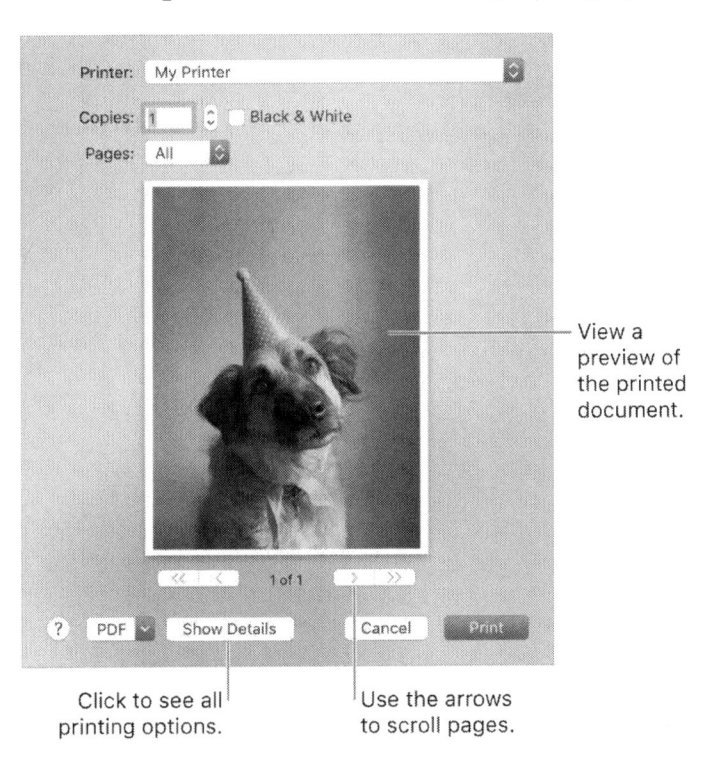

View a preview of the printed document.

Click to see all printing options.

Use the arrows to scroll pages.

Tip: To view a full-size preview in the Preview app, click the PDF pop-up menu, then choose Open PDF in Preview.

2. If the settings in the Print dialog are fine as is, click Print, and you're done. Otherwise, continue to step 3.

3. Choose any of the following common print settings (you may need to click Show Details to see some of the settings):

    o *Printer:* Choose the printer you want to use. If the printer you want isn't available, you can add one. If you see an icon next to the printer you want to use, there may be an issue you need to resolve—.

    o *Presets:* A preset is a group of print settings. In most cases you can use the default settings, but you can also choose a group of settings you've saved from a previous print job.

    o *Copies:* Specify the number of copies you want. To print all pages of a document before the next copy prints, click Show Details, click the print options pop-up menu, choose Paper Handling, then select "Collate pages."

    o *B & W (or Black and White):* Select to print in black and white, if your printer has this capability.

- *Two-Sided:* Select this to print on both sides of the paper (also called *duplexing*), if your printer has this capability.

- *Pages:* Choose to print all pages, a single page, or a range of pages.

- *Orientation:* Click the buttons to switch between portrait or landscape orientation.

For more detailed information about printing options, you might see different options in the Print dialog depending on your printer and the app you're using. If these instructions differ from what you're seeing, check the documentation for the app you're using by clicking Help in the menu bar.

If you print a document and see unexpected margin sizes or clipped text, there may be a conflict between the margins set for your page size in the app and the nonprintable area of the page set for your selected printer. Try setting the nonprintable area for the page size to zero.

Organize files in stacks on Mac

You can use stacks on the desktop to keep files neatly organized in groups. Whenever you save a file to the desktop, it's automatically added to the appropriate stack, helping to keep your desktop clean. The Dockincludes a Downloads stack to group files you download from the internet.

Use stacks on the desktop

You can group stacks by kind (such as images or PDFs), date (such as Date Created or Date Last Opened), or Finder tags. For example, all the documents on your desktop can be grouped in one stack while screenshots are grouped in another.

On your Mac, do any of the following:

- *Turn on stacks:* Click the desktop, then choose View > Use Stacks or press Control-Command-0. You can also Control-click the desktop, then choose Use Stacks.

- *Browse files in a stack:* Swipe left or right on the stack using two fingers on the trackpad; use one finger on a Magic Mouse. You can open the top file in a stack by double-clicking it.

- *Open or close a stack:* Click the stack. You can double-click a file to open it.

- *Change how stacks are grouped:* Click the desktop, choose View > Group Stacks By, then choose an option, such as Date Added. Or Control-click the desktop, choose Group Stacks By, then choose an option.

- *Change how stacks look:* Click the desktop, choose View > Show View Options, then change options. Or Control-click the desktop, then choose Show View Options. You can make icons bigger, change the spacing between icons, move icon labels to the side, or show more information (such as how many files are in a stack).

Use stacks in the Dock

The Dock comes with a Downloads stack where you can easily access items you download from the internet, receive as attachments, or accept using AirDrop.

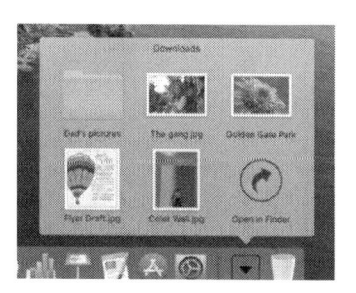

You can add files and folders to the Dock for quick access, and even display them as a stack. Your Mac creates an alias to the file or folder.

On your Mac, do any of the following:

- *Add files and folders:* Drag and drop a folder to the right of the separator line (after recently used apps, if shown).

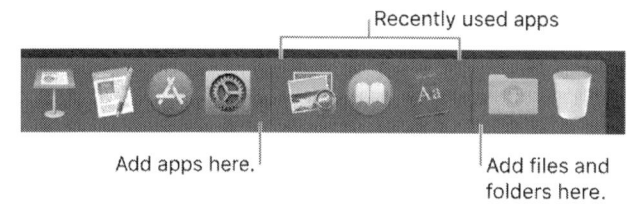

- *Open or close a file or folder:* Click it. When a folder is open, double-click any item to open it. To see a folder in the Finder, click Open in Finder.

- *Change how folders look:* Control-click the folder, then choose how the items in it are sorted, whether to show it in the Dock as a folder or a stack, and how to view its content (such as in a grid or fan).

Organize files in folders on Mac

Everything on your Mac—documents, pictures, music, apps, and more—is organized in folders. As you create documents, install apps, and do other work, you can create new folders to keep yourself organized.

Create a folder

1. On your Mac, click the Finder icon in the Dock to open a Finder window, then navigate to where you want to create the folder.

   Alternatively, click the desktop if you want to create the folder on the desktop.

2. Choose File > New Folder, or press Shift-Command-N.

   If the New Folder command is dimmed, you can't create a folder in the current location.

3. Enter a name for the folder, then press Return.

Move items into folders

1. On your Mac, click the Finder icon in the Dock to open a Finder window.

2. Do any of the following:

   - *Put an item in a folder*: Drag it to the folder.

- *Put several items in a folder:* Select the items, then drag one of the items to the folder.

  All selected items move to the folder.

- *Keep an item in its original location and put a copy in a folder:* Select the item, press and hold the Option key, then drag the item to the folder.

- *Keep an item in its original location and put an alias for it in a new folder:* Press and hold the Option and Command keys, then drag the item to the folder to create the alias.

- *Make a copy of an item within the same folder:* Select the item, then choose File > Duplicate or press Command-D.

- *Copy files to a different disk:* Drag the files to the disk.

- *Move files to a different disk:* Press and hold the Command key, then drag the files to the disk.

Quickly group multiple items into a new folder

You can quickly create a folder of items on the desktop or in a Finder window.

1. On your Mac, select all the items you want to group together.

2. Control-click one of the selected items, then choose New Folder with Selection.

3. Enter a name for the folder, then press Return.

Merge two folders with the same name

If you have two folders with identical names at two different locations, you can merge them into a single folder.

- On your Mac, press and hold the Option key, then drag one folder to the location that contains a folder with the same name. In the dialog that appears, click Merge.

   The Merge option appears only if one of the folders contains items that are not in the other folder. If the folders contain different versions of identically named files, the only options are Stop or Replace.

To organize your files automatically, use Smart Folders. Smart Folders automatically gather files by type and subject matter, and are instantly updated as you change, add, and remove files on your Mac.

Use tags to organize files on Mac

You can tag files and folders to make them easier to find. Tags work with all your files and folders, whether you store them on your Mac or keep them in iCloud.

Ask Siri. Say something like: "Find files that are tagged red."

Tag files and folders

You can add multiple tags to any file or folder.

On your Mac, do any of the following:

- *Tag an open file:* Hold the pointer to the right of the document title, click the arrow, click in the Tags field, then enter a new tag, or choose one from the list.

- *Tag a new file when you save it:* Click File > Save. In the Save dialog, click in the Tags field, then enter a new tag, or choose one from the list.

- *Tag a file on the desktop or in the Finder:* Select the item, then open the File menu. You can also Control-click the item, or tap it with two fingers. Choose a color below Tags, or click Tags to choose from more tags or enter a new tag.

  In a Finder window, you can also select the item, click the Tags button, then enter a new tag, or choose one from the list.

Tip: Use keyboard shortcuts to tag files quickly—select a file, then use Control-1 through Control-7 to add (or remove) your favorite tags. Control-0 (zero) removes all tags from a file.

Find items you tagged

1. On your Mac, click the Finder icon in the Dockto open a Finder window.

2. Do any of the following:

- *Search for a tag:* Enter the tag color or name in the search field, then select the tag from the suggestions.

- *Select a tag in the sidebar:* To see everything with a certain tag, click the tag ⬤ in the Finder sidebar.

  To change the items you see in the sidebar, choose Finder > Preferences, click Tags, then select the tags you want to see.

- *Group items by a tag:* Click the Group button ▦, then choose Tags.

- *Sort items by a tag:* In any view, choose View > Show View Options, click the Sort by pop-up menu, then choose Tags. In List view, select the Tags checkbox to display the column, move the pointer over the Tags column, and then click it. Click the column name again to reverse the sort order.

Remove tags

On your Mac, do one of the following:

- *Remove tags from an item:* Control-click the item or tap it with two fingers, then click Tags. Select the tags you want to remove, then press Delete.

- *Remove tags from your Mac:* In the Finder, choose Finder > Preferences, then click Tags. Select the tags you want to remove, then click the Remove button .

Edit tags

1. In the Finder on your Mac, choose Finder > Preferences, then click Tags.

2. Do any of the following:

    - *See a tag in the Finder sidebar:* Select the blue checkbox to the right of the tag.

    - *Change a tag color:* Click the color next to the tag , then choose a new color.

    - *Change a tag name:* Click the tag, click the tag's name, and then enter a new name.

    - *Create a new tag:* Click the Add button .

    - *Delete a tag:* Select the tag, then click the Remove button .

- *Add a tag to the shortcut menu:* Select the tag in the list, then drag it over the tag you want to replace in the favorites section at the bottom of the window. There can be up to seven tags in the shortcut menu that appears when you Control-click a file.

- *Remove a tag from the shortcut menu:* Drag the tag out of the Favorite Tags section until you see the remove sign ⊗.

Back up your files with Time Machine on Mac

With Time Machine, you can back up your entire Mac, including system files, apps, music, photos, emails, and documents. When Time Machine is turned on, it automatically backs up your Mac and performs hourly, daily, and weekly backups of your files.

When you use Time Machine on a computer using Apple File System (APFS), Time Machine not only keeps a copy of everything on your backup disk, it also saves *local snapshots* of files that have changed on your internal disk, so you can recover previous versions. These local snapshots are saved hourly (unless you deselect Back up automatically) and they're stored on your computer's internal disk.

Note: If you're using APFS, local snapshots are created on your APFS disk, regardless of whether the disk is on a portable or desktop Mac.

If you accidentally delete or change a file, you can use Time Machine to recover it.

Click arrows to navigate through backups.

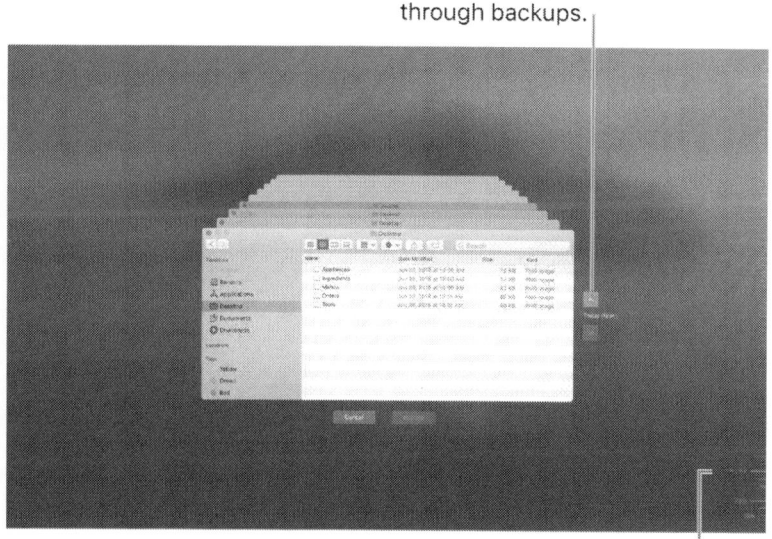

Backup timeline

Even though Time Machine creates local snapshots on computers using APFS, you should also back up your files to a location other than your internal disk, such as an external hard disk, a disk on your network, or a Time Capsule. That way, if anything ever happens to your internal disk or to your Mac, you can restore your entire system to another Mac.

1. Connect an external hard disk to your Mac and turn the disk on.

You're asked if you want to use the disk to back up your Mac.

2. On your Mac, click Use as Backup Disk, then follow the instructions in Time Machine preferences.

   To open Time Machine preferences, choose Apple menu > System Preferences, then click Time Machine.

Note: If you create a backup on a Mac or partition with macOS Catalina, you can only use that backup on Mac computers or partitions with macOS Catalina.

Restore items backed up with Time Machine on Mac

If you use Time Machine to back up the files on your Mac, you can easily get back lost items or recover older versions of files. You can use Time Machine within many apps.

1. On your Mac, open a window for the item you want to restore.

   For example, to recover a file you accidentally deleted from your Documents folder, open the Documents folder. To recover an email message, open your inbox in Mail.

   If you're missing an item from the desktop, you don't need to open a window.

2. Use Launchpad to view and open apps on Mac and open Time Machine. A message may appear while your Mac connects to the backup disk.

You can also open Time Machine by clicking the Time Machine icon ⏰ in the menu bar, then choosing Enter Time Machine. If the Time Machine icon isn't in the menu bar, choose Apple menu > System Preferences, click Time Machine, then select "Show Time Machine in menu bar."

3. Use the arrows and timeline to browse the local snapshots and backups.

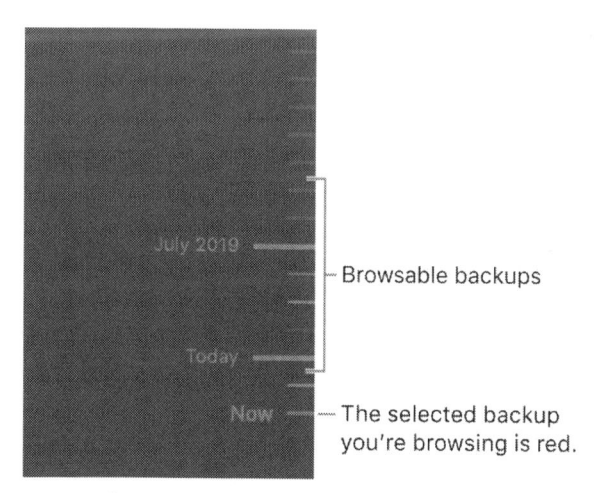

- Browsable backups
- The selected backup you're browsing is red.

If you see a pulsing light to semi-dark gray tick mark, it represents a backup that's still loading or validating on the backup disk.

4. Select one or more items you want to restore (these can include folders or your entire disk), then click Restore.

Restored items return to their original location. For example, if an item was in the Documents folder, it's returned to the Documents folder.

With many apps, you can use Time Machine within individual documents, so you can examine and read past versions to find the version you want. You can use iCloud Drive and iCloud Photos to safely store your documents, photos, and videos in iCloud.

Chapter 8
Apple ID and iCloud
Create an Apple ID on Mac

An Apple ID gives you access to the iTunes Store, the App Store, Apple Books, iCloud, FaceTime, and other Apple services. It consists of an email address (for example, michael_cavanna@icloud.com) and a password. Apple recommends you use the same Apple ID for all Apple services. For more information about Apple ID You can create an Apple ID using your current email address or have an @iCloud email address generated for you.

You can create an Apple ID on a Mac, an iOS or iPadOS device, or at the Apple ID account website. See the Apple Support article Sign in with your Apple ID.

Using either your current email address or an iCloud address generated for you, create an Apple ID:

1. On your Mac, choose Apple menu > System Preferences, then click Sign In.

2. Click Create Apple ID, then follow the onscreen instructions.

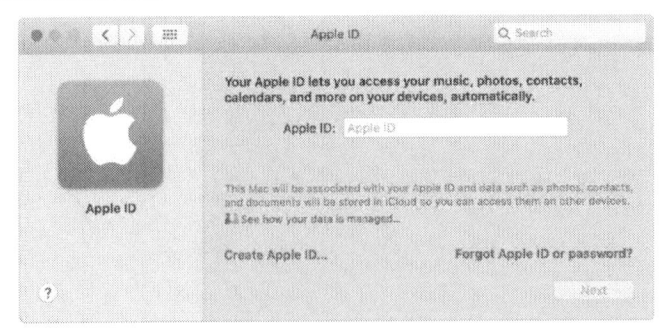

Note: In several countries and regions, you can use a phone number instead of an email address as your Apple ID. See the Apple Support article Use your mobile phone number as your Apple ID.

For information about setting up your Apple ID preferences on your Mac,

To keep your purchases and access to Apple services secure, don't share your Apple ID and password with others. To share your purchases with family members, you can set up a Family Sharing group with up to six members of your family.

For information about using your Apple ID on an iOS or iPadOS device, see "Manage Apple ID and iCloud settings" in the user guide for iPhone, iPad, or iPod touch.

Use two-factor authentication for security on your Mac, iOS devices, and iPadOS devices

Two-factor authentication is an extra layer of security for your Apple ID designed to ensure that you're the only one who can access your account—even if someone knows your password.

Turn on two-factor authentication for your Apple ID

Apple IDs created with macOS 10.12.4 or later, iOS 10.3 or later, or iPadOS are protected with two-factor authentication automatically. When you sign in to your account, you see that two-factor authentication is already on. If it is not on, you can turn on two-factor authentication while setting up a new Mac, or follow the steps below any time to turn it on in Password & Security preferences.

1. On your Mac, choose Apple menu > System Preferences, click Apple ID, then select Password & Security in the sidebar.

2. Click Set up Two-Factor Authentication, then click Continue.

3. Answer the verification questions, then click Verify.

4. Enter your phone number for verification, select a verification method, and then click Continue.

5. When asked, verify your identity with the six-digit verification code sent to your trusted phone. You won't be asked for a verification code again on your Mac unless you sign out your Apple ID completely, erase your Mac, or need to change your password for security reasons.

Sign in to a new device or browser with two-factor authentication

A verification code is a temporary code sent to your trusted devices or phone number when you sign in to a new device or browser with your Apple ID.

1. When you're asked for the verification code, look for a notification at a trusted phone number or on any of your trusted devices.

   To send the code to a trusted phone number, click "Didn't get a verification code?" in the notification, then choose the phone number.

2. On a trusted device, tap or click Allow to see the code on that device.

3. Enter the code on your Mac.

Get a verification code on a Mac, even when it's offline

If you can't receive a verification code on your phone or trusted devices, or if none of them are available, you can get a verification code in Password & Security preferences, even if your Mac is offline.

1. On your Mac, choose Apple menu > System Preferences, click Apple ID, then select Password & Security in the sidebar.

2. Click Get Verification Code.

3. Write down the verification code or enter it in the notification, then click OK.

Add a trusted device

To make a Mac (macOS 10.11 or later), an iOS device (iOS 9), or an iPadOS device a trusted device, you must sign in using your Apple ID on the Mac or device.

- *Adding a Mac (macOS Catalina):* Choose Apple menu > System Preferences, then click Sign In and enter your Apple ID. Follow the onscreen instructions.

- *Adding a Mac (macOS Mojave or earlier):* Choose Apple menu > System Preferences, click iCloud, then click Sign In and enter your Apple ID. Follow the onscreen instructions.

- *Adding an iOS or iPadOS device:* Tap Settings >*your name* at the top of the screen. (If you're using a device with iOS 10.2 or earlier, tap Settings > iCloud.) Verify your identity with a six-digit verification code.

    If you previously signed in to your Mac, iOS, or iPadOS device using a different Apple ID, sign out, then sign in again.

You won't be asked for a verification code again on that device unless you sign out of your Apple ID completely, erase your device, or need to change your password for security reasons.

Add or remove a trusted phone number

You must verify at least one trusted phone number to enroll in two-factor authentication.

1. On your Mac, choose Apple menu > System Preferences, click Apple ID, then select Password & Security in the sidebar.

2. Do any of the following:

   - To add a phone number, click the Add button ＋. Enter your Mac login password. Enter a phone number that can be used to verify your identity. Select whether you want to be reached by text or phone call, then click Continue. Enter the code sent to the email address or phone number and click next. Your trusted phone numbers appear in a list.

   - To remove an email or phone number, select a phone number, click the Delete button —, and then click Remove.

View or remove trusted devices

1. On your Mac, choose Apple menu > System Preferences, then click Apple ID.

   A list of your trusted devices appears at the bottom of the sidebar.

2. Do any of the following:

   - *View details of a trusted device:* Select a device in the list to see details about it.
   - *Remove a trusted device:* Select a device in the list, click Remove from Account, then click Remove.

If you already use two-factor authentication, you can no longer turn it off. Certain features in the latest versions of iOS, iPadOS, and macOS require this extra level of security. If you recently updated your account to turn on two-factor authentication and then decide not to use it, you must stop using it within 2 weeks. Open your enrollment confirmation email and click the link to return to your previous security settings.

You can manage your trusted devices and phone numbers by signing in to your Apple ID account page.

Set up your Apple ID preferences

Use your Apple ID to sign in to your Apple ID preferences. Your Apple ID gives you access to all Apple services, including iTunes Store, Book Store, App Store, iCloud, and other Apple services. After you sign in, you can use Apple ID preferences to change your account name, photo, contact information, password and security settings, payment and shipping information, and more.

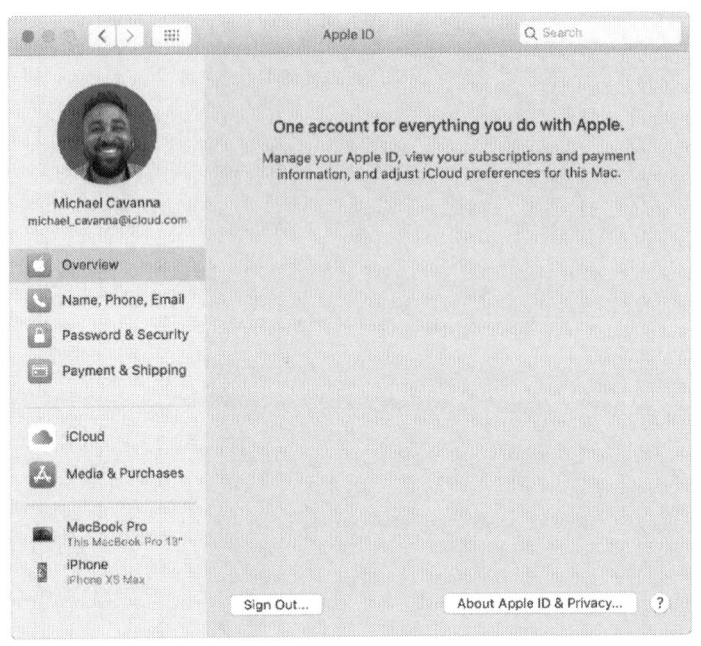

Use the following sidebar items to set up your Apple ID preferences on your Mac:

- *Overview:* Use these options to review Apple ID & Privacy policy and sign out of your Apple ID. *Name, Phone, Email:* Use these options to enter your name, phone number, email information, and other contact information associated with your Apple ID.

- *Password & Security:* Use these options to change the password and security settings associated with your Apple ID.

- *Payment & Shipping:* Use these options to set up the payment and shipping information associated with your Apple ID.

- *ICloud:* Use these options to select the iCloud features you want and manage iCloud storage.

- *Media & Purchases:* Use these options to change the media and purchases settings associated with your Apple ID.

- *Trusted devices:* Use this list to review the trusted devices that use your Apple ID and select and change a trusted device's options.

Set up iCloud features on Mac

At any time after you sign in to your Apple ID, you can select the iCloud features you want to use.

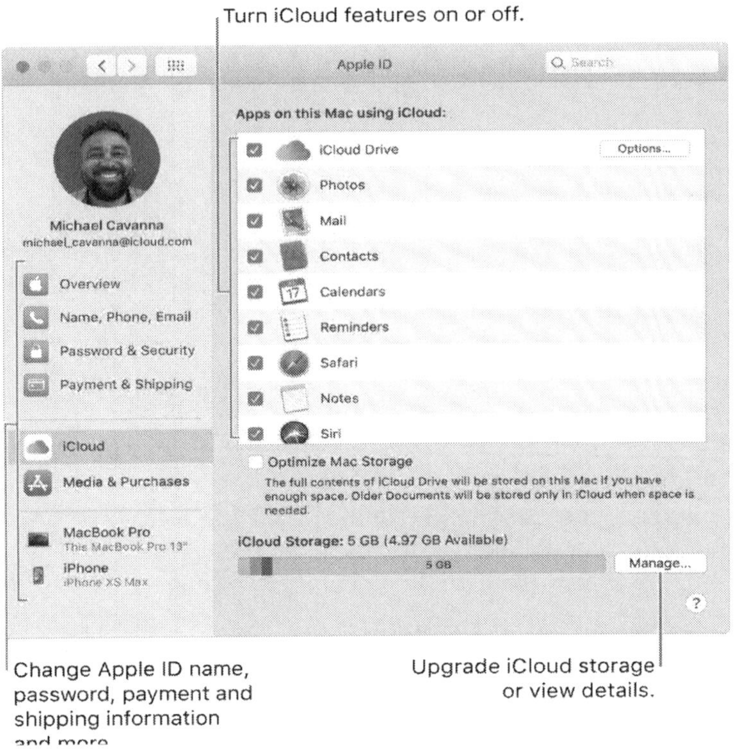
Turn iCloud features on or off.
Apple ID
Apps on this Mac using iCloud:
iCloud Drive
Options...
Photos
Mail
Contacts
Calendars
Reminders
Safari
Notes
Siri
Michael Cavanna
michael_cavanna@icloud.com
Overview
Name, Phone, Email
Password & Security
Payment & Shipping
iCloud
Media & Purchases
MacBook Pro
iPhone
Optimize Mac Storage
The full contents of iCloud Drive will be stored on this Mac if you have enough space. Older Documents will be stored only in iCloud when space is needed.
iCloud Storage: 5 GB (4.97 GB Available)
5 GB
Manage...
Change Apple ID name, password, payment and shipping information and more
Upgrade iCloud storage or view details.

Important: To set up Messages in iCloud to share all your messages across devices, open Messages on your Mac, choose Messages > Preferences, click I Message, then select the Enable Messages in iCloud checkbox. To set up iCloud features on your iOS or iPadOS device, Apple TV, or Windows computer, see the Apple Support article Change your iCloud feature settings.

Turn iCloud features on or off

1. On your Mac, choose Apple menu > System Preferences, click Apple ID, then select iCloud in the sidebar.

2. Select the app whose iCloud features you want to use. Deselect any app whose iCloud features you don't want to use.

   Some features have additional settings you can change by clicking Options or Details near the feature name when the feature is turned on.

   If you select the Contacts feature while your Contacts app is synced with Google Contacts, Google syncing is turned off. You should keep it turned off while using iCloud for your contacts.

Turn on iCloud Photos

1. On your Mac, choose Apple menu > System Preferences, click Apple ID, then select iCloud in the sidebar.
2. Select Photos.

For more information about setting up iCloud in Photos,

Change iCloud Keychain options

If your Apple ID is set up for two-factor authentication you are done setting up iCloud Keychain when you select it in the iCloud apps list. When you set up iCloud on a new device, you can allow the device to use your iCloud data simply by entering the login password or passcode on a device that already has iCloud set up.

Follow the instructions below if a Options button appears beside the iCloud Keychain option.

1. On your Mac, choose Apple menu > System Preferences, click Apple ID, then select iCloud in the sidebar.

2. Click the Options button next to Keychain, and select any of the following:

    - Whether your iCloud Security Code can be used to approve iCloud Keychain on new devices.

    - The iCloud Security Code and the phone number used to verify your identity after you use the iCloud Security Code.

3. If "Waiting for approval" appears below Keychain, click Options to enter your iCloud Security Code instead of approving this Mac from another device.

Change Find My Mac details

1. On your Mac, choose Apple menu > System Preferences, click Apple ID, then select iCloud in the sidebar.

2. If "Location Services is off" appears below Find My Mac, click Details, then follow the onscreen instructions so you can locate this Mac.

To set up iCloud on your iOS or iPadOS device, or Windows computer, see the Apple Support article Set up iCloud on your iPhone, iPad, or iPod touch.

Use iCloud Drive to store documents on your Mac, iPhone, and iPad

With iCloud Drive, you can safely store all kinds of documents in iCloud, and access them from all your computers, and iOS and iPadOS devices. If you like, you can have all the files in your desktop and documents folders stored automatically in iCloud Drive. That way, you can save files right where you usually keep them, and they become available on all your computers, and iOS and iPadOS devices.

You can use iCloud Drive on Mac computers (OS X 10.10 or later), iOS devices (iOS 8 or later), iPadOS devices, and Windows computers with iCloud for Windows (Windows 7 or later required). You must be signed in to iCloud using the same Apple ID on all your computers and devices.

You can also use iCloud Drive on iCloud.com from a web browser on a Mac or Windows computer.

To set up iCloud drive using an iOS or iPadOS device, Windows PC, or on iCloud.com, see the Apple Support article Set up iCloud Drive.

Set up iCloud Drive

If you haven't yet set up iCloud Drive on this Mac, you can do it now in the iCloud pane of Apple ID preferences.

1. On your Mac, choose Apple menu > System Preferences, click Apple ID, then select iCloud in the sidebar.
2. Select iCloud Drive.

The first time you select the iCloud Drive feature on any of your devices, you're asked to upgrade. When you upgrade, your documents and data currently stored in iCloud are moved to iCloud Drive. If you're not asked to upgrade, your account is already upgraded.

Important: After upgrading to iCloud Drive, your documents stored in iCloud Drive are only available on your computers, and iOS and iPadOS devices that meet minimum system requirements, and have iCloud Drive turned on. Your documents in iCloud Drive are also available on iCloud.com.

If you have devices with iCloud Drive turned off, documents and data on those devices aren't kept up to date with documents and data on your devices with iCloud Drive turned on.

Store your Desktop and Documents folders in iCloud Drive

1. On your Mac, choose Apple menu > System Preferences, click Apple ID, select iCloud in the sidebar, then click Options next to iCloud Drive.

   If you don't see Options next to iCloud Drive, make sure iCloud Drive is turned on.

2. Select Desktop & Documents Folders.

3. Click Done.

After you select Desktop & Documents Folders, you're Desktop and Documents folders are moved into iCloud Drive. They also appear in the iCloud Drive section of the Finder sidebar.

If you can't move or save a document to iCloud Drive

If you can't move or save a document to iCloud Drive, your iCloud storage space may be full. The document stays on your Mac, and is uploaded to iCloud Drive when space becomes available.

ICloud Drive shares your iCloud storage with iCloud Photos, iOS and iPadOS device backups, messages and attachments in iCloud Mail (your @icloud.com email account), and more.

To get more space, do the following:

- Upgrade your storage. Remove items you don't need to store in iCloud Drive.

Use iCloud File Sharing to share documents with other iCloud users

With iCloud File Sharing, you can share any kind of file or document in iCloud Drive with other iCloud users. You and the people you invite can view and even work on your documents. The people who receive your invitation can click a link to download the shared file from iCloud to any of their devices. Everyone views the same shared document. If you allow others to make edits, they can change and save the document and you see the updates the next time you open the document on your Mac.

For information about iCloud Drive and setting it up on your Mac.

Share documents

1. To share a document, do one of the following:

   o In the Finder on your Mac, select iCloud Drive, select a document, click the Share button, then choose Add People.

   Tip: If the item is on the desktop, Control-click it, choose Share from the shortcut menu, then choose Add People.

- In an app that supports iCloud File Sharing, open a document, click the Share button, then choose Add People.

2. Select the app you want to use to send the invitation.

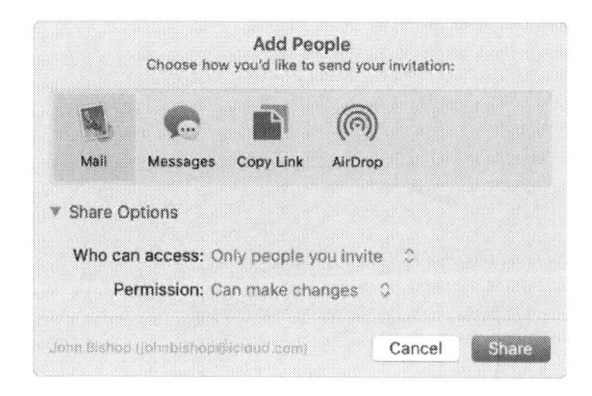

You can use Mail, Messages, Copy Link, and Airdrop to send an invitation.

3. Click the disclosure triangle next to Share Options, click the "Who can access" pop-up menu, then do one of the following:

    - Choose "Only people you invite" to allow only invitees to access the document.
    - Choose "Anyone with link" to allow anyone who receives the link to access the document. For example, your invitees can share the link and give access to others not included in the original invitation.

4. Click the Permission pop-up menu, then do one of the following:

    - Choose "Can make changes" to allow others to revise the document.
    - Choose "View only" to allow read-only access.

5. Click Share, then add the email addresses of the people you want to share with.

When the invitees receive your invitation, they can download the shared file from iCloud to any of their devices. If you allow it, they can make changes and save the document. You see the updates the next time you open the file on your Mac.

Accept an invitation and revise a document

When you download a document that you've been invited to share, the shared file is available in iCloud Drive on your Mac, the Files app (iOS 11 or later or iPadOS) or the iCloud Drive app (on a device with iOS 10 or earlier or iPadOS), on iCloud.com, and on a PC with iCloud for Windows.

If you have permission to revise the document, you can open it with any compatible app, then make and save your changes.

1. In the invitation, click the link to the shared document.

    If necessary, sign in with your Apple ID and password.

2. When the file opens in an app on your Mac, make your changes, then save the document.

You can also open the file later with any compatible app and make changes. Anyone sharing the document sees the latest changes to the file the next time they open it.

Change the sharing options of a document

You can change the sharing settings you chose after you share a document.

1. On your Mac, select the document in iCloud Drive, or open it in an app that supports iCloud File Sharing, click the Share button, then choose Show People.

2. Do any of the following:

    - *Share a document with more people:* Click the Add People button, then add an email address for each new invitee.

    - *Copy a link to the shared file to send to another person:* Click the disclosure triangle next to Shared Options, then click Copy Link. You can now paste the link into an email or other app.

    - *Change who can access the file to download:* Click the disclosure triangle next to Share Options, then choose "Only people you invite" to only allow invitees to access the document, or choose

"Anyone with link" to allow anyone who receives the link to access the document.

- *Change whether the shared document can be changed or viewed only:* Click the disclosure triangle next to Share Options, then choose "Can make changes" to allow others to revise the document, or choose "View only" to allow read-only access.

- *Change the sharing settings for a specific person:* Position the pointer over a person's name, click ⋯ , then choose the settings you want.

- *Stop sharing a file with a specific person:* Position the pointer over the person's name, click ⋯ , then choose Remove Access.

Stop sharing a document

You can stop sharing files with people you invited.

1. On your Mac, select the document in iCloud Drive or open it in an app that supports iCloud File Sharing.

2. Click the Share button ⬆, then choose Show People.

3. Do any of the following:

- *Stop sharing with everyone:* Click the disclosure triangle next to Share Options, then click Stop Sharing.

- *Stop sharing with a specific person:* Hold the pointer over the person's name, click ⋯, then choose Remove Access.

You can also simply move or delete the document from iCloud Drive to stop others from having access to it.

Use iCloud File Sharing to share documents with other iCloud users

With iCloud File Sharing, you can share any kind of file or document in iCloud Drive with other iCloud users. You and the people you invite can view and even work on your documents. The people who receive your invitation can click a link to download the shared file from iCloud to any of their devices. Everyone views the same shared document. If you allow others to make edits, they can change and save the document and you see the updates the next time you open the document on your Mac.

For information about iCloud Drive and setting it up on your Mac.

Share documents

1. To share a document, do one of the following:

- In the Finder on your Mac, select iCloud Drive, select a document, click the Share button, then choose Add People.

  Tip: If the item is on the desktop, Control-click it, choose Share from the shortcut menu, then choose Add People.

- In an app that supports iCloud File Sharing, open a document, click the Share button, then choose Add People.

2. Select the app you want to use to send the invitation.

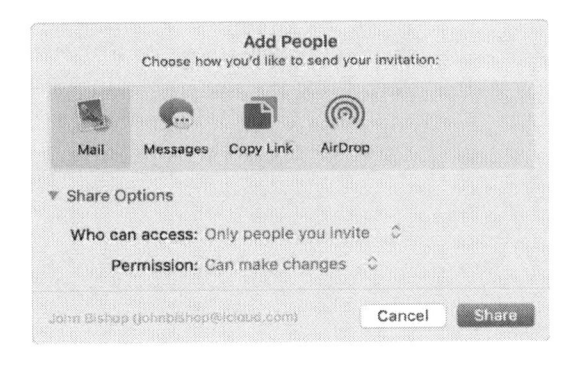

You can use Mail, Messages, Copy Link, and Airdrop to send an invitation.

3. Click the disclosure triangle next to Share Options, click the "Who can access" pop-up menu, then do one of the following:

- Choose "Only people you invite" to allow only invitees to access the document.

- Choose "Anyone with link" to allow anyone who receives the link to access the document. For example, your invitees can share the link and give access to others not included in the original invitation.

4. Click the Permission pop-up menu, then do one of the following:

    - Choose "Can make changes" to allow others to revise the document.

    - Choose "View only" to allow read-only access.

5. Click Share, then add the email addresses of the people you want to share with.

When the invitees receive your invitation, they can download the shared file from iCloud to any of their devices. If you allow it, they can make changes and save the document. You see the updates the next time you open the file on your Mac.

Accept an invitation and revise a document

When you download a document that you've been invited to share, the shared file is available in iCloud Drive on your Mac, the Files app (iOS 11 or later or iPadOS) or the iCloud Drive app (on a device with iOS 10 or earlier or iPadOS), on iCloud.com, and on a PC with iCloud for Windows.

If you have permission to revise the document, you can open it with any compatible app, then make and save your changes.

1. In the invitation, click the link to the shared document.

   If necessary, sign in with your Apple ID and password.

2. When the file opens in an app on your Mac, make your changes, then save the document.

   You can also open the file later with any compatible app and make changes. Anyone sharing the document sees the latest changes to the file the next time they open it.

Change the sharing options of a document

You can change the sharing settings you chose after you share a document.

1. On your Mac, select the document in iCloud Drive, or open it in an app that supports iCloud File Sharing, click the Share button, then choose Show People.

2. Do any of the following:

   - *Share a document with more people:* Click the Add People button, then add an email address for each new invitee.

- *Copy a link to the shared file to send to another person:* Click the disclosure triangle next to Shared Options, then click Copy Link. You can now paste the link into an email or other app.

- *Change who can access the file to download:* Click the disclosure triangle next to Share Options, then choose "Only people you invite" to only allow invitees to access the document, or choose "Anyone with link" to allow anyone who receives the link to access the document.

- *Change whether the shared document can be changed or viewed only:* Click the disclosure triangle next to Share Options, then choose "Can make changes" to allow others to revise the document, or choose "View only" to allow read-only access.

- *Change the sharing settings for a specific person:* Position the pointer over a person's name, click ⊙, then choose the settings you want.

- *Stop sharing a file with a specific person:* Position the pointer over the person's name, click ⊙, then choose Remove Access.

Stop sharing a document

You can stop sharing files with people you invited.

1. On your Mac, select the document in iCloud Drive or open it in an app that supports iCloud File Sharing.

2. Click the Share button, then choose Show People.

3. Do any of the following:

   - *Stop sharing with everyone:* Click the disclosure triangle next to Share Options, then click Stop Sharing.

   - *Stop sharing with a specific person:* Hold the pointer over the person's name, click, then choose Remove Access.

You can also simply move or delete the document from iCloud Drive to stop others from having access to it.

Manage iCloud storage on Mac

When you sign up for iCloud, you automatically get 5 GB of free storage. Your iCloud storage is used for documents stored in iCloud Drive, iCloud Photos, iOS and iPadOS device backups, messages and attachments in iCloud Mail (your @icloud.com email account), and more. If you run out of space, you can upgrade your storage. You can also remove stored items to make more space available.

View and manage iCloud storage

1. On your Mac, choose Apple menu > System Preferences, click Apple ID, then select iCloud in the sidebar.

2. Click Manage, then do any of the following:

   o *Upgrade your storage:* Click Buy More Storage or Change Storage Plan, choose the amount of storage you want, then follow the instructions.

   When you buy an iCloud storage upgrade, it's billed to your Apple ID account. If you're in a Family Sharing group and you use the same Apple ID to share family purchases, the upgrade is billed to the family organizer's account.

   o *See how an app or feature is using storage:* Select an app or feature on the left, then read the usage information on the right.

   o *Remove an iOS or iPadOS device backup:* Click Backups on the left, select a device on the right whose backup you don't need, then click Delete (below the list of backups). If you don't see Backups on the left, your iOS or iPadOS device doesn't have iCloud backups.

WARNING: If you delete the iCloud backup for your current iOS or iPadOS device, iCloud stops automatically backing up the device.

- *Turn off Siri and remove Siri-related data:* Select Siri on the left, then click Disable and Delete.

3. Click Done.

Delete items from iCloud storage

You can permanently remove all documents and data for an app, remove documents individually, and also recover files you deleted from iCloud Drive in the last 30 days. You can save copies of documents before removing them from iCloud.

Use iCloud Photos to store photos in iCloud

With iCloud Photos, all the photos and videos in your photo library are stored in iCloud, so you can access them from your Mac, PC, iPhone, iPad, or Apple TV, and on iCloud.com.

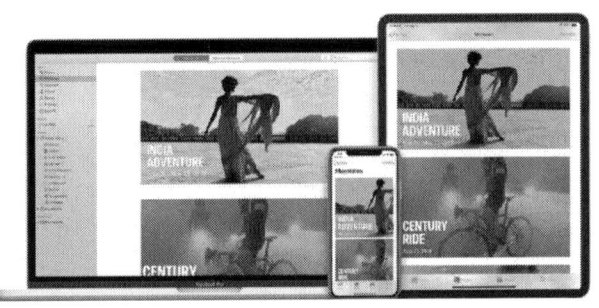

Any new photos and videos you add to Photos, or take with an iPhone or iPad, appear on all your devices that have iCloud Photos turned on. Your photos and albums are organized the same way on every device, and if you make edits or remove items, you see the changes on all your devices.

Before you set up iCloud Photos, update to the latest version of macOS, or the latest version of iOS or iPadOS on your device.

Turn on iCloud Photos

If you're not already signed in with your Apple ID, choose Apple menu > System Preferences, click "Sign in," then enter your Apple ID and password. Click iCloud in the Apple ID preferences sidebar, then select Photos in the list of apps.

1. In the Photos app on your Mac, choose Photos > Preferences, then click iCloud.

2. Select the iCloud Photos checkbox.

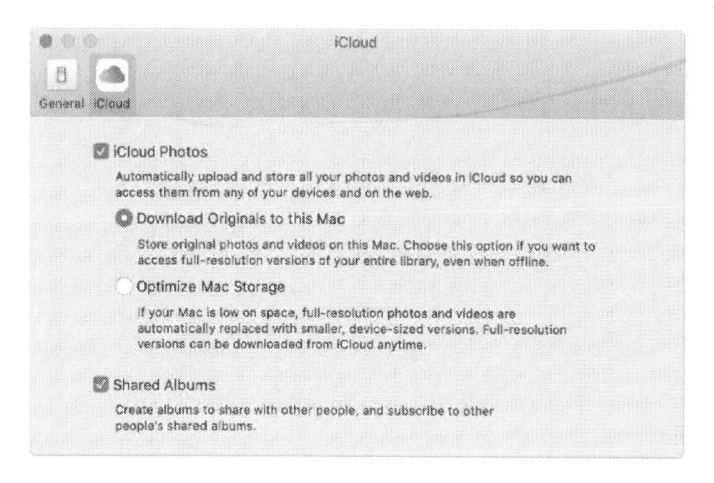

3. Select one of the following options:

- *Download Originals to this Mac:* Stores the full-size versions of your photos both on your Mac and in iCloud.

- *Optimiz Mac Storage:* Stores smaller versions of your photos on your Mac when storage space is limited, and keeps the original, full-size photos in iCloud. Choose this option to conserve space on your Mac. To restore the originals to your Mac, just select "Download Originals to this Mac."

    Note: If this option is selected and you run low on storage space, only the still image of a Live Photo is stored on your Mac. When you open a Live Photo, the video portion is downloaded from iCloud so you can play it.

When you first turn on iCloud Photos, it can take a while to upload your photos to iCloud. You can continue to use Photos while your photos are being uploaded.

Tip: To temporarily pause uploading or downloading of photos and videos with iCloud Photos, click Photos in the sidebar, click Days in the toolbar, then click the Pause button at the bottom of the Days view. Photos pauses uploading and downloading for 24 hours and then resumes automatically.

ICloud Photos doesn't store your projects or Smart Albums in iCloud or on your iPhone or iPad. (Smart Albums are shared with your other Mac computers, however.) To keep a backup of your projects and Smart Albums, make sure you back up the library to another storage device.

You can have multiple photo libraries, but iCloud Photos keeps only the photos and videos in the System Photo Library up to date.

Stop using iCloud Photos

Important: If you turn off iCloud Photos, you'll be prompted to select "Download Originals to this Mac" in the iCloud pane of Photos preferences so that all your original photos can be downloaded to your Mac. Be sure to allow time for your originals to download before turning off iCloud Photos.

1. In the Photos app on your Mac, choose Photos > Preferences, then click iCloud.
2. Deselect the iCloud Photos checkbox.
3. If you want to turn off iCloud Photos on all your devices, open Apple ID preferences in System Preferences, select iCloud in the sidebar, click the Manage button, click Photos, then click "Turn off and Delete."

After you turn off iCloud Photos on your Mac, edits you make to photos on your Mac don't appear on your other devices, and new photos and videos you take aren't added to Photos on your

Mac. Your library remains in iCloud and available to other devices that use iCloud Photos.

If you don't use iCloud Photos on your Mac, you can sync your Mac and a connected iPhone or iPad to transfer photos..

WARNING: If you turn off iCloud Photos on all your devices, your photos and videos will be deleted from iCloud in 30 days, and you won't be able to recover them, unless you click Undo Delete before that time.

Chapter 9
Family and Friends
Set up Family Sharing on Mac

Family Sharing lets up to six members of your family share iTunes Store, App Store, and Apple Books purchases, an iCloud storage plan—all without sharing accounts. Your family can share subscriptions to Apple Music, Apple TV, Apple News+, and Apple Arcade (not available in all countries or regions). Your family can also share a photo album, a family calendar, and help locate each other's' devices with the Find My app on theMac, on iCloud.com, and on iOS and iPadOS devices.

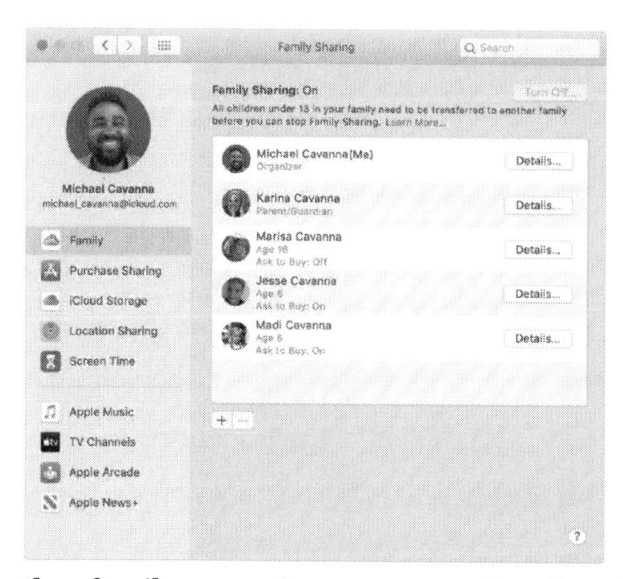

One adult—the family organizer—sets up Family Sharing and invites up to five people to join the Family Sharing group.

Choose Apple menu > System Preferences, and do one of the following:

- *If you have signed in to your Apple ID:* Click Family Sharing.

- *If you have not signed in to your Apple ID:* Click Sign In. Enter your Apple ID information according to the onscreen instructions.

  After signing in, click ⚟ at the top of the System Preferences window, then click Family Sharing, which now appears next to the Apple ID preferences.

2. Select Family in the sidebar.

3. To add yourself as the family organizer and add family members to your Family Sharing group, click the Add button ➕, then do one of the following:

   - *Add someone who has an Apple ID:* Enter the name or email address of the person you want to join the family, click Continue, then follow the onscreen instructions.

     If the person you're adding is nearby, they can simply enter their Apple ID and password.

Otherwise, you can email the person an invitation to join.

- *Create an Apple ID for a child under 13:* Select "Create an Apple ID for a child who doesn't have an account," click Continue, then follow the onscreen instructions.

4. To add another member, repeat step 3.

5. To select the apps and services that you want your family to share, do any of the following:

    - *Set up Purchase Sharing:* Select Purchase Sharing in the sidebar, then select your options. Your family can share purchases from the iTunes Store, the App Store, and Apple Books so everyone has access to them. All purchases are made through the shared payment method you set up. You can change the account used to make purchases and decline to share your purchases with family members.

    - *Upgrade your iCloud Storage:* Select iCloud Storage in the sidebar, then click Upgrade to upgrade your iCloud storage plan, from 200 GB to 2 TB. Family members can share the plan with you or keep their own individual storage plans.

- *Set up Location Sharing:* Select Location Sharing in the sidebar, then click Learn More to learn how to set up location sharing on all your devices. You can set up location sharing so that all family members can view each other's locations in the Find My app and Messages. You can use the Find My app on your Mac, iCloud.com, iOS and iPadOS devices.

- *Screen Time:* Select Screen Time in the sidebar, click Open Screen Time Settings, then select the options you want.

- *Subscribe to Apple Music:* Select Apple Music in the sidebar. If you don't have an Apple Music Family plan subscription, you can subscribe for a free 14-day trial. When you subscribe to an Apple Music family membership, all family members get unlimited access to Apple Music automatically.

- *Subscribe to TV Channels:* Select TV Channels in the sidebar. If you don't have a TV channel subscription, click Learn More to learn about TV channel subscriptions. When a family member subscribes, all family members get unlimited access to TV Channels automatically.

- *Subscribe to Apple News+:* Select Apple News+ in the sidebar. If you don't have Apple News+ subscription, click Learn More to learn about Apple News+ subscriptions. When a family member subscribes, all family members get unlimited access to Apple News+ automatically.

- *Subscribe to Apple Arcade (not available in all countries or regions):* Select Apple Arcade in the sidebar. If you don't have an Apple Arcade subscription, click Learn More to learn about Apple Arcade subscriptions. When a family member subscribes, all family members get unlimited access to Apple Arcade automatically.

Before purchases are available to all family members, each person must confirm the Apple ID they use to share the iTunes Store, the App Store, and Apple Books purchases.

Set up Screen Time for a child on Mac

The most flexible and convenient way to set up and manage Screen Time for a child is by using Family Sharing. When you use Family Sharing, you can remotely manage and monitor each child's device usage from your own account on any Mac, iPhone, or iPad. However, if you aren't using Family Sharing, you can still set up Screen Time for a child by logging in to their Mac account.

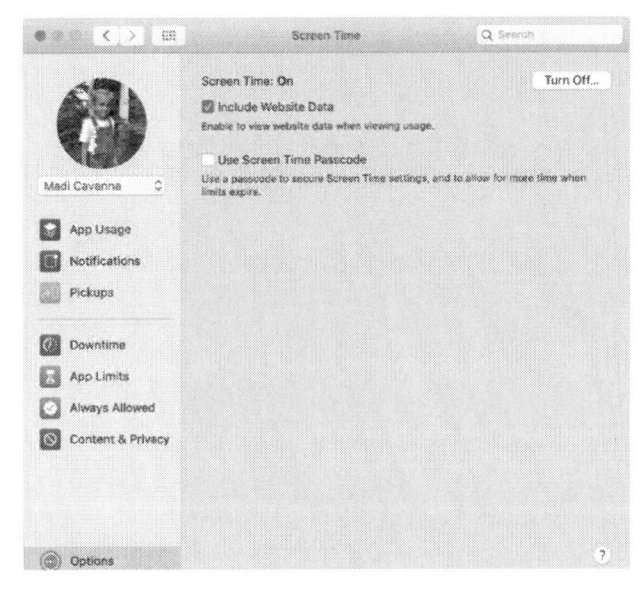

1. On your Mac, do one of the following:

    - *If you're using Family Sharing:* Log in to your account, then make sure you're signed in with your Apple ID.

    - *If you aren't using Family Sharing:* Log in to the child's account.

2. Choose Apple menu > System Preferences, then click Screen Time .

3. If you're using Family Sharing, click the pop-up menu in the sidebar, then choose a child.

4. Click Options in the lower-left corner of the sidebar.

5. Click Turn On in the upper-right corner.

6. Select any of the following options:

    - *Include Website Data:* Select this option if you want Screen Time reports to include details about the specific websites visited. If you don't select this option, websites are just reported as Safari usage.

    - *Use Screen Time Passcode:* Select this option to keep Screen Time settings from being changed, and to require a passcode to allow additional time when limits expire.

7. If you want to, do any of the following:

    - Click Downtime in the sidebar, then set up a downtime schedule.

    - Click App Limits in the sidebar, then set time limits for apps and websites.

    - Click Always Allowed in the sidebar, then choose apps that can be used at any time.

    - Click Content & Privacy in the sidebar, then set up content & privacy restrictions.

Share purchases with others in your Family Sharing group

As a family member, you have immediate access to purchases that other family members share with each other. You can download their purchases on your computer, and iOS and iPadOS devices at any time. You can let other family members access your purchases in the same way. You can hide individual purchases you don't want other family members to share.

Before you can share family purchases, you must join a family and set up Purchase Sharing.

View and download purchases made by other family members

1. Go to the Purchased section in Music, the App Store, or Apple Books.

   - *In Music:* Choose Account > Purchased. If you don't see that menu command, choose Account > Sign In.
   - *In App Store:* Choose Store > View My Account.
   - *In Books:* Choose Store > Book Store Home, then click Purchased below Quick Links on the right.

2. Click your name or choose a family member to view their purchases.

3. Download the items you want.

When a family member initiates a purchase, it's billed directly to the family organizer's account. Once purchased, the item is added to the initiating family member's account and is shared with the rest of the family. If the family organizer ever stops

Family Sharing, each person keeps the items they chose to purchase—even if they were paid for by the family organizer.

Hide a purchase from other family members

You can hide your individual Music, App Store, and Apple Books purchases so they aren't available to other family members.

1. Go to the Purchased section of Music, the App Store, or Apple Books.

    - *In Music:* Choose Account > Purchased. If you don't see that menu command, choose Account > Sign In.

    - *In App Store:* Choose Store > View My Account.

    - *In Books:* Choose Store > Book Store Home, then click Purchased below Quick Links on the right.

2. Do one of the following:

    - *In Music:* Select the type of content you want to hide, place the pointer over the item you want to hide, then click its Remove button ⊗.

    - *In App Store:* Position the pointer over the item you want to hide, click ⋯, and then choose Hide Purchase.

- *In Books:* Place the pointer over the item you want to hide, then click its Remove button ⊗.

Stop hiding a purchase

You can reveal individual Music, App Store, and Apple Books purchases that you have hidden so that they are available to other family members.

1. Go to the Account Information section in Music, the App Store, or Apple Books.

    - *In Music:* Choose Account > View My Account. If you don't see that menu command, choose Account > Sign In.

    - *In App Store:* Choose Store > View My Account. If you don't see that menu command, choose Store > Sign In.

    - *In Books:* Choose Store > View My Apple ID. If you don't see that menu command, choose Store > Sign In.

2. Do one of the following:

    - *In Music:* Scroll to Hidden Purchases, click Manage, and then click Unhide for the item.

- In App Store: Click View information. In the hidden items section, click Manage, then click Unhide for the item.

- In Books: Scroll to Hidden Purchases, click Manage, and then click Unhide for the item.

Stop sharing your purchases

1. On your Mac, choose Apple menu > System Preferences, click Family Sharing, then select Purchase Sharing in the sidebar.
2. Deselect Share My Purchases under your Account information.

Note: To share purchases, family members must be in the same iTunes Store country or region. If a family member changes their iTunes Store country or region, that person might lose access to other family members' purchases, and installed apps that were shared from other family members might not work.

Ways to share calendars on Mac

Share your calendar with friends and family

Share iCloud calendars with others who also have iCloud accounts. You can choose whether others can edit the calendar or only view it.

Share your calendar with coworkers

Share individual calendars or share calendar accounts with people who use the same calendar service. For example, if you share an Exchange or CalDAV server at work, you can choose whether coworkers can edit your calendar account or only view it.

Share a read-only version of your calendar with anyone

Publish a calendar to a web server or at a specific web address. Others can view the calendar on the web and subscribe to it using Calendar. Subscribers can view your calendar but they can't edit it.

Stop sharing a calendar

You can stop sharing or publishing any of your calendars. See the topics linked above.

Share a reminder list on Mac

You can share reminder lists in your upgraded iCloud reminders account with other iCloud users who've also upgraded their reminders. Everyone who shares the list can create and edit reminders from any computer or device set up with iCloud. Notifications aren't shared; you can set a reminder to remind you at a time or place, but it won't remind anyone else.

After you start sharing a reminder list, you can add or remove people, or stop sharing the list with anyone.

Note: All Reminders features described in this guide are available when using upgraded iCloud reminders. Some features aren't available when using accounts from other providers.

Share a list

1. In the Reminders app on your Mac, choose View > Show Sidebar.

2. Select a reminder list in the sidebar, then click the Share button .

3. In the Add People window, choose how you'd like to send your invitation:

    - *Send invitation using Mail or Messages:* Click Mail or Messages, click Share, enter the people you want to share the list with, then click Send.

    - *Send invitation using a link or AirDrop:* Click Copy Link or AirDrop, enter addresses or phone numbers of the people you want to share the list with, then click Share.

The invitee must accept the invitation in order to view and edit the shared list.

Add people to a shared list

After you start sharing a reminder list, you can add more people who can see the list.

1. In the Reminders app on your Mac, choose View > Show Sidebar.

2. Select a reminder list in the sidebar, then click the Share button.

3. In the People window, click Add People.

4. In the Add People window, choose how you'd like to send your invitation:

    - *Send invitation using Mail or Messages:* Click Mail or Messages, click Share, enter the people you want to share the list with, then click Send.

    - *Send invitation using a link or Airdrop:* Click Copy Link or Airdrop, enter addresses or phone numbers of the people you want to share the list with, then click Share.

Remove people from a shared list

If you no longer want to share a list with a person, you can remove them from the shared list.

1. In the Reminders app on your Mac, choose View > Show Sidebar.

2. Select a reminder list in the sidebar, then click the Share button.

3. In the People window, select the person you want to remove.

4. Click the More Options button ⋯ at the right, then choose Remove Access.

5. Click Done.

When you remove a person from the shared list, the list is removed from all of the other person's devices.

Stop sharing a list

If you change your mind about sharing a list or no longer need to share it, you can stop sharing it with everyone.

1. In the Reminders app on your Mac, choose View > Show Sidebar.

2. Select a reminder list in the sidebar, then click the Share button.

3. In the People window, click Stop Sharing, then click Continue.

When you stop sharing a list, the list is removed from all participants' devices.

Create a shared album in Photos on Mac

After you turn on Shared Albums, it's easy to create a shared album to share your photos and video clips.

Create a shared album

1. In the Photos app on your Mac, select the photos and video clips you want to share.

2. Click the Share button in the toolbar and choose Shared Albums, then click New Shared Album.

3. Type a name for the shared album, then type the email addresses of the people you want to share the album with.

   If you want subscribers to be able to view the shared album from an iPhone or iPad, be sure to use the email addresses they use to sign in with their Apple ID.

4. Click Create.

Your invitees are sent an email asking them to subscribe to your shared album.

View a shared album

1. In the Photos app on your Mac, click a shared album under Shared in the sidebar.

   You can also click Shared in the sidebar to see all your shared albums in the window, then double-click a shared album to view it.

2. Click ‹ to see all your shared albums again.

Stop sharing an album

You can stop sharing an album with specific people by removing them from the subscribers list. To stop sharing a photo album entirely, you can delete it.

WARNING: When you delete a shared album, it's immediately removed from your devices and your subscribers' devices. If you think your subscribers might want to keep any photos or video from the album, you should alert them to save the items before you delete the shared album. Also, make sure you've downloaded any photos and videos that others have added to the album and that you want to keep. The photos you shared aren't deleted from your Photos library.

In the Photos app on your Mac, do one of the following:

- Click a shared album in the sidebar, click in the toolbar, and then click Delete Shared Album.

- Control-click the shared album you want to stop sharing, then choose Delete Shared Album.

View activity in your shared albums

To see the latest activity in your shared albums—including photos that have been recently added and who added them—use the Activity album, in your shared albums.

Click to view the entire shared album.

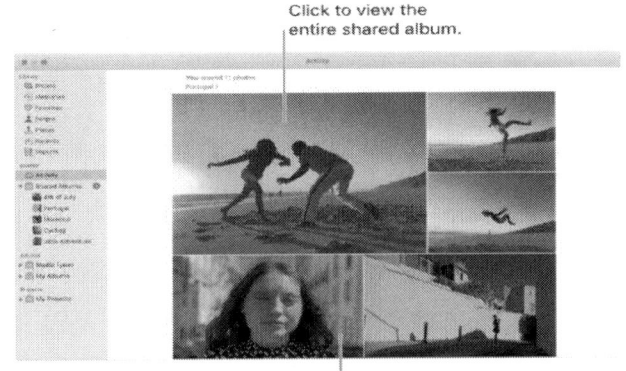

In the Activity album, you see the most recent sharing

- In the Photos app on your Mac, click Activity below Shared in the sidebar, then scroll to view changes.

Locate a friend in Find My on Mac

After you start following a friend, you can see and label their locations, contact them through Messages, FaceTime, or email, and get directions to where they are.

Ask Siri. Say something like: "Where's John Bishop?" In the Find My app on your Mac, click People.

1. In the People list, select a name.

    - *If your friend can be located:* They appear on a map so you can see where they are.

    - *If your friend can't be located:* You see "No location found" below their name.

- *If you aren't following your friend:* You see "Can see your location" below their name. Ask to follow a friend to see their location.

2. Click the Info button ⓘ on the map, then do any of the following:

    - *Label a friend's location:* Click Edit Location Name, then select an option (such as Home or Gym), or click Add Custom Label, enter a name, then press Return.

      The label appears below your friend's name instead of the location information.

    - *Contact a friend:* Click Contact, then choose an option.

    - *Get directions to a friend's location:* Click Directions.

      The Maps app opens with the directions from your location to your friend's location.

    - *Set up notifications*

Chapter 10
Privacy and Security

Learn how passwords are used on MacOS is designed to give you a safe and secure computing environment. The security of your Mac depends a great deal on using secure passwords in key areas.

Login password

A login password, also called a *user password*, allows you to log in and access the information on your Mac. When you create your login password, be sure it's easily memorable, write it down, and keep it in a secure location. Privileges are limited by the type of user. An administratoruser is required to perform many important tasks, such as setting certain system preferences, installing software, and administering standard users.

Apple ID

An Apple ID gives you access to the iTunes Store, the App Store, Apple Books, iCloud, FaceTime, and other Apple services. It consists of an email address (for example, michael_cavanna@icloud.com) and a password. Apple recommends you use the same Apple ID for all Apple services. When you create your Apple ID password, be sure it's easily memorable, write it down, and keep it in a secure location. You can also use your Apple ID to reset your login password if you forget it. Sign in to your Apple ID account page.

Passwords in iCloud Keychain

Keeping track of passwords is hard, especially if you follow the best practice of never using the same password twice and have multiple devices. ICloud Keychain keeps website and Wi-Fi passwords up to date across your Mac, iOS devices, and iPadOS devices. It also keeps account passwords and settings that you add to Internet Accounts preferences up to date on your Mac.

When you need to create a new password for a website, Safari suggests a unique, hard-to-guess password and saves it in your iCloud Keychain. Safari fills it in automatically the next time you need to sign in, so you don't have to remember it or enter it on any of your devices. It's recommended that you use the suggested strong password presented by Safari when creating passwords for websites and internet apps. If you don't use a suggested strong password and need help with a password for a website later, see the website's help, or the account information on the website.

If you need help with a password for an app that connects to an account on the internet or a network, see the documentation that came with the app, or online information that supports the app. For example, if you have a mail account with a service provider or website, see the documentation on the website or contact the provider.

Passwords in Keychain Access

Keychain Access stores passwords for various apps and services, and saves you the effort of authenticating separately for each of the items in your keychain. The keychain is secured by a keychain password, which is unlocked when a user logs in.

Recovery key

When you encrypt the information on your Mac using File Vault, you can create a recovery key. If you forget your login password, you can use the recovery key to unlock your startup disk and change the login password. The recovery key should not be stored in the same location as the Mac, where it can be discovered.

Manage passwords using keychains on Mac

MacOS uses keychains to help you keep track of and protect the passwords, account numbers, and other confidential information you use every day on your Mac computers and iOS and iPadOS devices.

You can use the Keychain Access app on your Mac to view and manage your keychains. When you use iCloud Keychain, you can keep your passwords and other secure information updated across your devices.

What is a keychain?

A keychain is an encrypted container that securely stores your account names and passwords for your Mac, apps, servers, and websites, and confidential information, such as credit card numbers or bank account PIN numbers.

When you access a website, email account, network server, or other password-protected item, you can choose to save the password in your keychain so you don't have to remember or enter the password each time.

Each user on a Mac has a login keychain. The password for your login keychain matches the password you use to log in to your Mac. If an administrator on your Mac resets your login password, you'll need to reset your login keychain password.

Keychain Access

You use the Keychain Access app on your Mac to view and manage your login and other keychains, and also the items securely stored in the keychains—for example, keys, certificates, passwords, account information, and notes. If you forget a password, you can find it in Keychain Access.

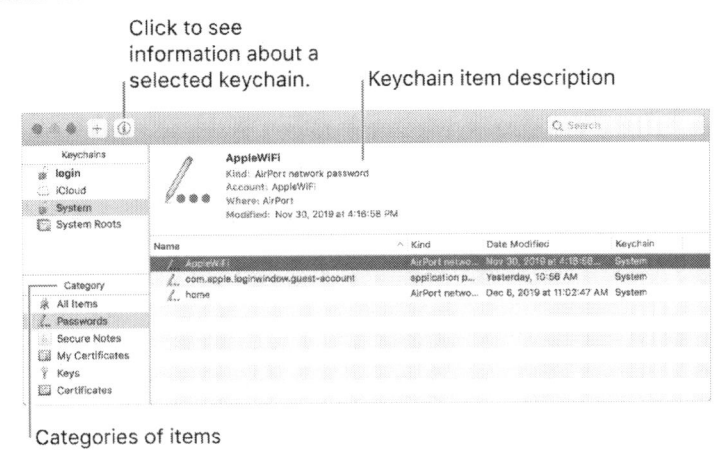

ICloud Keychain

If you use iCloud, you can have iCloud Keychain securely store the website login information and credit card information you use with AutoFill in Safari, and your Wi-Fi network information. ICloud Keychain automatically keeps that information up to date across all your Mac computers and iOS and iPadOS devices. ICloud Keychain also stores login information for the accounts you use in Mail, Contacts, Calendar, and Messages so it's available on all your devices.

Tip: When you use passwords and credit cards online, you can let Safari store them in your keychain and automatically fill them in for you. If you also use iCloud Keychain on your Mac and iOS and iPadOS devices, Safari can fill in the stored information on any of your devices.

Reset your Mac login password

Sometimes a login password needs to be reset—for example, if you have forgotten the login password and can't use a password hint to remember it.

When a user's login password is reset, a new default keychain is created to store the user's passwords.

Reset your login password using your Apple ID

If you associated your user account with your Apple ID, you can use your Apple ID to reset your login password.

1. On your Mac, choose Apple menu > Restart, or press the Power button on your computer and then click Restart.

2. Click your user account, click the question mark in the password field, then click the arrow next to "reset it using your Apple ID."

3. Enter an Apple ID and password, then click next.

   Follow the instructions to reset your login password.

Reset your login password using a recovery key

If you turned on File Vault encryption and created a recovery key, you can use the recovery key to reset your login password.

1. On your Mac, choose Apple menu > Restart, or press the Power button on your computer and then click Restart.
2. Click your user account, click the question mark in the password field, then click the arrow next to "reset it using your recovery key."
3. Enter the recovery key, then click next.

   Follow the instructions to reset your login password.

Reset the password of another user

An administrator can reset the passwords of other users.

1. On your Mac, choose Apple menu > System Preferences, then click Users & Groups.
2. Click the lock icon to unlock it, then enter an administrator name and password.
3. Select a user, then click Reset Password.

Set up your Mac to be secure

Here are some things you can do to make your Mac more secure.

Use secure passwords

To keep your information safe, you should use passwords to secure your Mac, and choose passwords that can't be easily guessed.

Require users to log in

If others can get physical access to your Mac, you should set up separate users for each person using the Mac, and require each user to log in. This prevents an unauthorized person from using the Mac. It also separates user files, so users only have access to their own personal files and settings. Users cannot see or modify the files or settings of other users.

Secure your Mac when it's idle

You can set your Mac to log out the current user if the Mac has been inactive for a certain period of time. You should also require a password to wake it from sleep or from the screen saver. For convenience, you can set up a hot corner to click whenever you want to immediately lock your screen.

Limit the number of administrative users

One or more people can have administrator privileges for a Mac. By default the administrator is the person who initially set up the Mac.

Administrators can create, manage, and delete other users, install and remove software, and change settings. For these reasons, an administrator should create a standard user account to use when administrator privileges are not needed. If the security of a standard user is compromised, the potential harm is far more limited than if the user has administrator privileges. If multiple people use your Mac, limit the number of users with administrator privileges.

Encrypt the data on your Mac with File Vault

If you have private or confidential information on your Mac, you can use File Vault encryption to protect that information from being seen or copied. File Vault encodes the information stored on your Mac so it is locked and cannot be read unless the login password is entered.

Guard your privacy on Mac

Privacy is an important concern when using apps that exchange information across the internet. MacOS includes security features to enhance your privacy and control the amount of information that's exposed about you and your Mac over the internet.

Use Screen Time

You can use Screen Time to monitor your children's computer use and limit their access to websites

Choose Apple menu > System Preferences, then click Screen Time.

Use the privacy features in Safari

Safari provides numerous features to help you control your privacy on the internet. You can browse privately, so Safari doesn't keep a record of websites you visited or items you downloaded. You can block pop-up windows, stop sites from storing cookies on your Mac, and more.

Control the personal information you share with apps

Location Services lets apps, such as web browsers, gather and use information based on your location. You can turn off Location Services completely, or you can select which apps can see information about your location.

Some apps may gather and use information from your contacts, photos, calendar, or reminders. Some apps may access the microphone or camera on your Mac.

Choose whether to share analytics information

You can help Apple improve the quality and performance of its products and services. MacOS can automatically collect analytics information from your Mac and send it to Apple for analysis. The information is sent only with your consent and is submitted anonymously to Apple. To choose whether analytics data is sent to Apple, use the Privacy pane of Security & Privacy preferences.

Choose Apple menu > System Preferences, click Security & Privacy, click Privacy, and then click Analytics.

Set up a firewall

You can use a firewall to protect your privacy by blocking unwanted network communications with your Mac. If the firewall is turned on, you can also use "stealth mode," which prevents your Mac from being discovered by others on the web.

To set up and customize your firewall, use the Firewall pane of Security & Privacy preferences.

Choose Apple menu > System Preferences, click Security & Privacy, then click Firewall.

Protect your Mac from malware

MacOS has many features that help protect your Mac and your personal information from malicious software, or malware. One common way malware is distributed is by embedding it in a harmless-looking app.

You can reduce this risk by using software only from reliable sources. The settings in Security & Privacy preferences allow you to specify the sources of software installed on your Mac.

1. On your Mac, choose Apple menu > System Preferences, click Security & Privacy, then click General.

2. Click the lock icon to unlock it, then enter an administrator name and password.

3. Select the sources from which you'll allow software to be installed:

    - *App Store:* Allows apps only from the Mac App Store. This is the most secure setting. All the developers of apps in the Mac App Store are identified by Apple, and each app is reviewed before it's accepted. MacOS checks the app before it opens the first time to be certain it hasn't been modified since the developer shipped it. If there's ever a problem with an app, Apple removes it from the Mac App Store.

    - *App Store and identified developers:* Allows apps from the Mac App Store and apps from identified developers. Identified developers are registered with Apple and can optionally upload their apps to Apple for a security check. If problems occur with an app, Apple can revoke its authorization. MacOS checks the app before it opens the first time to be certain it hasn't been modified since the developer shipped it.

In addition to apps, other types of files may not be safe. Scripts, web archives, and Java archives have the potential to cause harm to your system. Of course, not all files like this are unsafe, but you should exercise caution when opening any such downloaded file. An alert appears when you first try to open these files.

Use Sign in with Apple on Mac

Sign in with Apple uses your Apple ID to securely create an account with an app or website—no need to fill out a form, verify your email address, or choose a new password—and simplifies signing in each time.

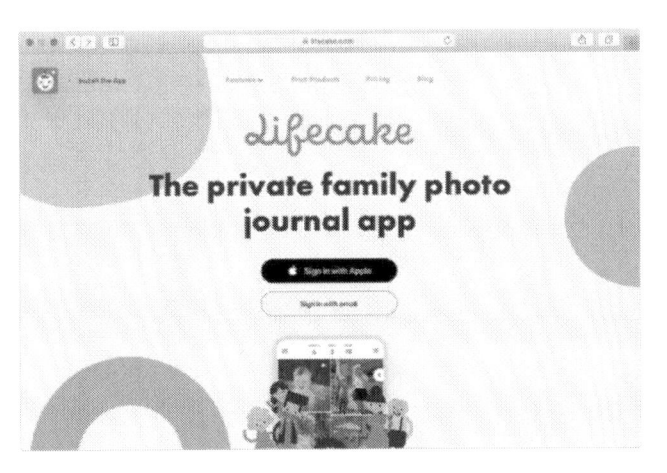

Create an account for an app or website

1. On your Mac, when you're asked to create an account for an app or a website, click Sign in with Apple, if available.

2. Follow the onscreen instructions, keeping the following in mind:

    - If you don't want to use your real name, click the Name field, then enter a different name.
    - If you have more than one email address associated with your Apple ID in Apple ID

preferences, choose which email to use for the app or website.

- If you prefer to keep your email address private, click Hide My Email. Apple generates a random and unique email address that's used to forward emails from the app or website to your real email address.

Sign in to your account for an app or website

1. On your Mac, click Sign in with Apple.
2. Enter your login password on your Mac (you may need to enter your Apple ID password instead) or, if you're Mac has Touch ID, use Touch ID.

You can also sign in from your other devices—iPhone, iPad, Apple Watch, and Apple TV—where you're signed in with the same Apple ID.

Change the address used to forward email from apps and websites

If you chose to hide your email when you created an account, and you have more than one email address associated with your Apple ID in Apple ID preferences, you can change the address that receives forwarded email.

1. On your Mac, choose Apple menu > System Preferences, then click Apple ID.

2. In the sidebar, click "Name, Phone, Email," then click Edit next to Hide My Email.

3. Choose a different email address, then click done.

Change Sign in with Apple settings for an app or website

1. On your Mac, choose Apple menu > System Preferences, then click Apple ID.

2. In the sidebar, click Password & Security, then click Edit next to Apps Using Your Apple ID.

3. Click an app or website in the sidebar, then do any of the following:

    o *Turn off forwarding email:* Click Turn Off. You won't receive any further emails from the app or website.

    o *Stop using Sign in with Apple:* Click Stop Using Apple ID. You may be asked to create a new account the next time you try to sign in with the app or website.

Clear your browsing history in Safari on Mac

You can remove all records that Safari keeps of where you've browsed during a period of time you choose. If your Mac and your other devices have Safari turned on in iCloud preferences, your browsing history is removed from all of them. Clearing your browsing history in Safari doesn't clear any browsing histories kept independently by websites you visited.

1. In the Safari app on your Mac, choose History > Clear History, then click the pop-up menu.
2. Choose how far back you want your browsing history cleared.

When you clear your history, Safari removes data it saves as a result of your browsing, including:

- History of webpages you visited
- The back and forward list for open webpages
- Top Sites that aren't marked as permanent
- Frequently visited site list
- Recent searches
- Icons for webpages
- Snapshots saved for open webpages
- List of items you downloaded (downloaded files aren't removed)
- Websites added for Quick Website Search
- Websites that asked to use your location
- Websites that asked to send you notifications

- Websites with plug-in content you started by clicking a Safari Power Saver notice.

Manage cookies and website data in Safari on Mac

You can change options in Safari preferences so that Safari always accepts or always blocks cookies and website data.

In the Safari app on your Mac, choose Safari > Preferences, click Privacy, then do any of the following:

- *Prevent trackers from using cookies and website data to track you:* Select "Prevent cross-site tracking."

  Cookies and website data are deleted unless you visit and interact with the trackers' websites.

- *Always block cookies:* Select "Block all cookies."

  Websites, third parties, and advertisers can't store cookies and other data on your Mac. This may prevent some websites from working properly.

- *Remove stored cookies and data:* Click Manage Website Data, select one or more websites, then click Remove or Remove All.

  Removing the data may reduce tracking, but may also log you out of websites or change website behavior.

- *See which websites store cookies or data:* Click Manage Website Data.

Note: Changing your cookie preferences or removing cookies and website data in Safari may change or remove them in other apps.

Locate a device in Find My on Mac

In Find my, you can see the location of a missing device, and play a sound on it to help you find it.

Important: To be able to locate a missing device, you must add it in Find My before it's lost.

See the location of a device

1. In the Find My app on your Mac, click Devices.
2. In the Devices list, select the device you want to locate.
    - *If the device can be located:* It appears on the map so you can see where it is.
    - *If the device can't be located:* Below the device's name, "No location found" appears. If you want to be notified when the location is available, click the Info button on the map, then select Notify When Found. You receive a notification once it's located.

Play a sound on a device

1. In the Find My app on your Mac, click Devices.

2. In the Devices list, select the device you want to play a sound on, then click the Info button ⓘ on the map.

3. Click Play Sound. For Air Pods, if they're separated, you can click Left or Right to find them one at a time.

   - *If the device is online:* A sound starts after a short delay and gradually increases in volume, then plays for about two minutes. The device may also vibrate. For all devices except Air Pods, a Find My [*device*] alert also appears on the device's screen.

   - *If the device is offline:* For Air Pods, you receive a notification on your devices the next time your Air Pods are in range of one of your devices and the Find My app is open. For all other devices, the sound plays the next time the device connects to a Wi-Fi or cellular network.

If you find your device, you can turn off the sound before it stops automatically—just press any button or any key.

Get directions to a device

1. In the Find My app on your Mac, click Devices.

2. In the Devices list, select the device you want to get directions to, then click the Info button ⓘ on the map.

3. Click Directions.

The Maps app opens with the directions from your location to the device's current location.

Thank you for purchasing our user manual!

Printed in Great Britain
by Amazon